i

Napoleon Revealed

44 Famous Paintings & Quotes

author

Hannah Bancutey

Table of Content

Preface   ix

Napoleon Bonaparte   4

Chapter 1:   Paintings
1792 - 1804   First Consul

01	Lieutenant Colonel of the 1st Battalion of Corsica	7
02	Bonaparte at the Pont d'Arcole	9
03	Napoleon leading his Troops over the Bridge of Arcole	11
04	Battle of Rivoli	13
05	The Battle of the Pyramids	15
06	Napoleon Pardoning the Rebels at Cairo	17
07	Napoleon Visiting the Plague Victims of Jaffa	19
08	Napoleon and his General Staff in Egypt	21
09	Napoleon Before the Sphinx	23
10	Coup of 18 Brumaire	25
11	First Consul Napoleon Bonaparte	27
12	Napoleon Crossing the Alps	29
13	General Bonaparte and his Chief of Staff Berthier	31
14	Installation of the Council State	33
15	The Coronation of Napoleon	35
16	Napoleon in Coronation Robes	37
17	Napoleon on His Imperial Throne	39
18	Napoleon Reviewing the Guard in the Place du Carrousel	41
19	Emperor Napoleon in His Study at the Tuileries	43
20	The Distribution of the Eagle Standards	45

1804 - 1815 The Emperor

21 The Battle of Austerlitz   47

22 Napoleon Presenting Marie Schellincka a Medal   49

23 Battle of Jena   51

24 Napoleon on the Battlefield of Eylau   53

25 Napoleon at the Battle of Friedland   55

26 Napoleon at the Gates of Madrid   57

27 Battle of Wagram   59

28 Napoleon's Farewell to Josephine   61

29 On the Eve of the Battle of Borodino   63

30 Napoleon at the Battle of Borodino   65

31 Napoleon on the Borodino Heights   67

32 In Gorodnya - To Breakthrough or Retreat?   69

33 Eugène de Beauharnais and Napoleon in Russia   71

34 Napoleon's Retreat from Russia   73

35 Battle of Leipzig   75

36 Bidding Farewell to the Imperial Guard at Fontainebleau   77

37 Napoleon at Fontainebleau   79

1815 - 1821 Exile till Death

38 Napoleon Leaving the Island Elba   81

39 Napoleon at Waterloo   83

40 On the Evening of the Battle of Waterloo   85

41 Napoleon on Saint Helena   87

42 Napoleon on His Deathbed   89

43 Death of Napoleon   91

44 Napoleon's Tomb   93

Chapter 2: Quotes
1769 - 1821 Napoleon's Quotes

Popular Quotes   97

Thought-Provoking Quotes   111

War Quotes   126

Leadership, Politics and Power Quotes   130

Funny Quotes   144

Strategy Quotes   146

General Quotes   156

Chapter 3: Honorable Mentions
1748 - 1965 From Musicians to Dictators

Ludwig van Beethoven   199

Johann Wolfgang van Goethe   200

Jacques-Louis David   201

Adolf Hitler   202

Winston Churchill   203

Leo Tolstoy   204

Josephine de Beauharnais   205

Napoleon Bonaparte   206

Preface

Welcome to a captivating journey through the life and legacy of
Napoleon Bonaparte. This book is divided into three chapters,
44 paintings, 100 quotes and 8 honorable mentions to illuminate
Napoleon Bonaparte's rise to power, his complex character, and
his profound impact on history. As we explore his triumphs and
downfalls, in the following pages we invite you to delve into the
intricate tapestry of events that shaped his era and ponder the
indelible mark he left on the world.

Napoleon

« *It is not necessary to bury the truth.*
It is sufficient merely to delay it until nobody cares. »

— Napoleon Bonaparte

Napoleon Revealed

44 Famous

Paintings &

Quotes

Hannah Bancutey

Napoleon Bonaparte

Napoleon Bonaparte, born on August 15, 1769, in Corsica, emerged as a towering figure in world history—a genius propagandist, statesman, and enigmatic leader of France. Rising from modest origins, he became a military prodigy during the French Revolution, ascending to power through political prowess and tactical brilliance.

As Emperor of the French, he reshaped Europe with his innovative policies, legal reforms, and vast territorial conquests. His military campaigns, marked by audacious strategies, altered the geopolitical landscape. Despite his remarkable achievements, his ambitions ignited conflicts that ultimately led to his downfall and exile. Napoleon's enduring legacy rests in his indelible impact on modern governance, military strategy, and the course of history.

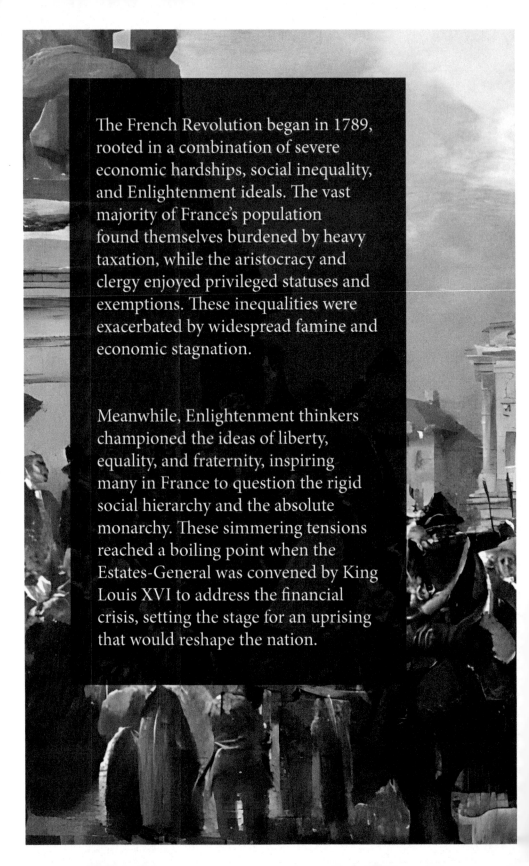

The French Revolution began in 1789, rooted in a combination of severe economic hardships, social inequality, and Enlightenment ideals. The vast majority of France's population found themselves burdened by heavy taxation, while the aristocracy and clergy enjoyed privileged statuses and exemptions. These inequalities were exacerbated by widespread famine and economic stagnation.

Meanwhile, Enlightenment thinkers championed the ideas of liberty, equality, and fraternity, inspiring many in France to question the rigid social hierarchy and the absolute monarchy. These simmering tensions reached a boiling point when the Estates-General was convened by King Louis XVI to address the financial crisis, setting the stage for an uprising that would reshape the nation.

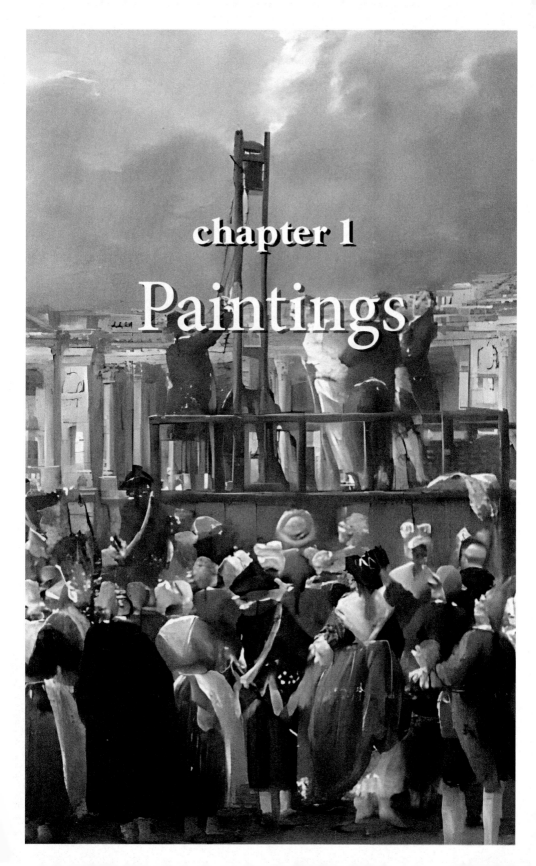

chapter 1
Paintings

Lieutenant Colonel of the 1st Battalion of Corsica (period: 1792)
by Felix Philippoteaux, 1834

Lieutenant Colonel of the 1st Battalion of Corsica

Felix Philippoteaux

Historically, the Lieutenant Colonel of the 1st Battalion of Corsica holds significance due to its portrayal of Napoleon Bonaparte's formative years as a military officer. During this period in the late 18th century, Corsica was grappling with shifting allegiances and revolutionary fervor. Napoleon's role within the Corsican National Guard and later in the French Revolutionary Army showcases his early leadership skills and strategic thinking. His experiences in Corsica during this time laid the groundwork for his subsequent rise to power in France and Europe. The historical context sheds light on the complex interplay between individual ambition, regional politics, and the broader currents of the French Revolution, all of which played a crucial role in shaping Napoleon's trajectory and impact on history.

The historically intriguing aspect of "Lieutenant Colonel of the 1st Battalion of Corsica" by Félix Philippoteaux offers a visual glimpse into Napoleon's formative years as a military officer during a time of political upheaval in Corsica and France. The painting captures Napoleon's early ambitions, leadership, and role within the Corsican National Guard, setting the stage for his later rise as a prominent figure in the French Revolutionary Army. The artwork provides insight into the intersection of individual aspiration, regional dynamics, and revolutionary fervor that shaped Napoleon's journey from a Corsican officer to a transformative figure in European history.

Bonaparte at the Pont d'Arcole (period: 15-17 November 1796)
by Antoine-Jean Gros, 1796

Painting 02

Bonaparte at the Pont d'Arcole

Antoine-Jean Gros

Bonaparte at the Pont d'Arcole is historically captivating for its representation of a defining moment in Napoleon Bonaparte's career during the Italian Campaign of the French Revolutionary Wars. In 1796, during the Battle of Arcole, Napoleon showcased his audacious leadership by leading his troops across a bridge under heavy enemy fire. This daring move demonstrated his ability to inspire and rally his soldiers, ultimately securing a critical victory against the Austrians. The event underscored Napoleon's tactical brilliance and his capability to adapt and innovate under pressure. It became emblematic of his rising star as a military commander, highlighting his charisma, strategic acumen, and capacity to change the course of history through decisive actions. The Battle of Arcole stands as a testament to the transformative role of leadership and strategic thinking in shaping historical outcomes.

"Bonaparte at the Pont d'Arcole" by Antoine-Jean Gros is historically compelling for its portrayal of a pivotal moment in Napoleon Bonaparte's early military career. Created in 1796, the artwork vividly captures Napoleon's audacious leadership during the Battle of Arcole in 1796. Gros's attention to detail and dramatic composition convey the intensity of the battle as Napoleon leads his troops across a bridge under enemy fire. The painting offers a visceral depiction of the chaos, bravery, and determination that defined this crucial episode. Through his skillful brushwork, Gros brings to life the raw emotions and decisive actions that marked Napoleon's ascent, reflecting the intersection of personal courage and strategic brilliance that would shape his future prominence as a transformative leader on the world stage.

Napoleon leading his Troops over the Bridge of Arcole (period: 15-17 November 1796) by Horace Vernet, 1826

Painting 03

Napoleon leading his Troops over the Bridge of Arcole

Horace Vernet

Napoleon leading his troops over the bridge of Arcole in 1796 is historically remarkable as it exemplifies his early military prowess and innovative tactics. During the Italian Campaign of the French Revolutionary Wars, Napoleon demonstrated his leadership and strategic brilliance by leading his soldiers across the bridge under heavy enemy fire, securing a critical victory against the Austrians. This audacious move showcased his ability to inspire and rally his troops in the face of adversity. The battle became Napoleon's defining moment in ascent, highlighting his daring and tactical acumen that would shape his subsequent military successes. The event underscores Napoleon's capacity to adapt and innovate, foreshadowing his later role as a transformative leader on the world stage and underscoring the intricate interplay between individual leadership and the course of history.

"Napoleon leading his Troops over the Bridge of Arcole" depicted by Vernet is historically striking for its visual portrayal of a crucial moment in Napoleon's early military career. The artwork captures the intensity and audacity of Napoleon's leadership during the Battle of Arcole. Vernet's attention to detail and dynamic composition convey the chaos and determination of the soldiers as they follow their resolute commander across the bridge under enemy fire. Through skillful brushwork, Vernet brings to life the energy and courage that characterized Napoleon's early successes, foreshadowing his later transformation into a world-renowned military strategist and political leader. The painting becomes a visual testament to the intersection of leadership, bravery, and tactical ingenuity that marked Napoleon's ascent, inviting viewers to witness a pivotal moment in his rise to power and its lasting impact on history.

Battle of Rivoli (period: 14-15 January 1797) by Felix Philippoteaux, ~19th century

Painting 04

Battle of Rivoli

Felix Philippoteaux

The Battle of Rivoli, fought in 1797 during the French Revolutionary Wars, is historically captivating for its pivotal role in Napoleon Bonaparte's rise to prominence. Commanding the French forces, Napoleon employed innovative tactics and strategic maneuvers to decisively defeat the Austrian army under General Alvinczy. The battle showcased Napoleon's remarkable ability to exploit the terrain and orchestrate complex movements, ultimately securing a significant victory for the French Republic. The triumph at Rivoli solidified Napoleon's reputation as a military genius and contributed to his ascent to becoming a prominent political and military leader in France. The battle's outcome marked a turning point in the conflict, highlighting the transformative impact of effective leadership, strategic thinking, and adaptability on the course of history.

The Battle of Rivoli by Félix Philippoteaux is historically captivating for its visual representation of a decisive moment in Napoleon Bonaparte's early military career. Created in the 19th century, the artwork vividly captures the intensity and dynamics of the battle fought in 1797 during the French Revolutionary Wars. Philippoteaux's attention to detail and dramatic composition convey the chaos, heroism, and strategic brilliance that marked the encounter. Through his skillful brushwork, Philippoteaux brings to life the raw emotions and pivotal actions that defined the battle, underscoring Napoleon's audacious leadership and tactical acumen. The painting serves as a visual testament to the convergence of courage, strategy, and historical significance, inviting viewers to witness a key episode in Napoleon's ascent and the transformative role of individual leadership in shaping the trajectory of events.

The Battle of the Pyramids (period: 21 July 1798) by Antoine-Jean Gros, 1810

Painting 05

The Battle of the Pyramids

Antoine-Jean Gros

The Battle of the Pyramids, fought in 1798 during the French Revolutionary Wars, is historically intriguing for its significance in Napoleon's conquest of Egypt. Part of his broader strategy to disrupt British trade routes and expand French influence, the battle saw French forces decisively defeating the Mamluk cavalry near the Pyramids of Giza. Napoleon's innovative tactics and disciplined troops allowed him to overcome the larger Mamluk forces, solidifying his reputation as a military genius. The battle's outcome underscored the effectiveness of modernized warfare against traditional methods, and it demonstrated Napoleon's capacity to adapt and prevail even in unfamiliar terrains. The event marked a notable chapter in Napoleon's career and contributed to the broader exploration and study of Egypt's ancient history and culture by European scholars.

"The Battle of the Pyramids" by Antoine-Jean Gros is historically captivating for its portrayal of a key moment in Napoleon Bonaparte's Egyptian campaign of 1798. The painting vividly captures the intensity of the battle between French forces and the Mamluk cavalry near the Pyramids of Giza. Gros's meticulous attention to detail and dramatic composition convey the chaos, heroism, and clash of cultures that defined the encounter. The artwork becomes a visual testimony to Napoleon's audacious military leadership and his ambition to expand French influence beyond Europe. Through Gros's brushwork, viewers are transported to the heart of a transformative era marked by exploration, imperial ambitions, and the melding of ancient history with contemporary conflicts, offering a window into the complex intersections of power, conquest, and cultural exchange on the world stage.

Napoleon Pardoning the Rebels at Cairo (period: October 1798) by Pierre-Narcisse Guérin, 1808

Painting 06

Napoleon Pardoning the Rebels at Cairo

Pierre-Narcisse Guérin

Napoleon Pardoning the Rebels at Cairo is historically intriguing as it reflects a defining moment during Napoleon Bonaparte's Egyptian campaign of 1798-1799. Following the capture of Cairo, Napoleon faced a challenging situation with local insurgents. By issuing a pardon to rebels who had resisted the French occupation, Napoleon aimed to consolidate his control over Egypt and gain local support. This gesture highlighted Napoleon's pragmatic approach to governance and his understanding of the political landscape. While it showcased his adaptability and willingness to negotiate, the event also highlighted the complexities of colonial rule and the delicate balance between asserting authority and maintaining order. Napoleon's actions in Cairo underscore the blend of military strategy, diplomacy, and local dynamics that defined his leadership, offering insights into his methods of asserting control and navigating the intricate sociopolitical fabric of the regions he sought to conquer.

"Napoleon Pardoning the Rebels at Cairo" by Guérin vividly portrays Napoleon's pragmatic approach to governance as he pardons local rebels who resisted French occupation. Guérin's attention to detail and emotive composition convey the convergence of power, diplomacy, and local dynamics, showcasing Napoleon's efforts to secure his rule by reconciling with insurgents. Through Guérin's artistic interpretation, viewers witness a pivotal instance of the delicate balance between asserting control and maintaining order in the midst of a complex colonial environment, reflecting Napoleon's multifaceted leadership style and the challenges inherent in maintaining dominance over distant territories.

Napoleon Visiting the Plague Victims of Jaffa (period: 11 March 1799) by Antoine-Jean Gros, 1804

Painting 07

Napoleon Visiting the Plague
Victims of Jaffa

Antoine-Jean Gros

"Napoleon Visiting the Plague Victims of Jaffa" is historically significant as it portrays a pivotal event during Napoleon Bonaparte's Egyptian campaign of 1799. The incident occurred after the French forces captured the city of Jaffa and faced an outbreak of bubonic plague among their ranks. In an attempt to boost the morale of his troops and project an image of compassionate leadership, Napoleon visited the afflicted soldiers at the plague hospital. However, this act has been surrounded by controversy, as accounts of the event vary. Some reports suggest that Napoleon may have exaggerated his involvement to enhance his heroic image, while others claim he took personal risks to show solidarity with his troops. This episode illustrates the challenges of leadership during military campaigns, the impact of disease on historical events, and the complexities of historical interpretation.

"Napoleon Visiting the Plague Victims of Jaffa" by Antoine-Jean Gros is remarkable for its evocative portrayal of a crucial moment in history. Gros masterfully employs dramatic lighting and composition to emphasize the stark contrast between the healthy figures surrounding Napoleon and the suffering soldiers lying on the ground. The emotional depth conveyed through the facial expressions and body language of the characters underscores the human toll of warfare. The work's skillful blending of historical narrative with emotional resonance creates a lasting impression, making it an artful exploration of compassion, leadership, and the complexity of historical interpretation.

Napoleon and his General Staff in Egypt (period: 1798 - 1799) by Jean-Léon Gérôme, 1867

Napoleon and his General Staff in Egypt

Jean-Léon Gérôme

Napoleon and his General Staff in Egypt hold historical significance for offering insights into Napoleon's leadership during his Egyptian campaign of 1798-1799. The interactions between Napoleon and his officers during this period shed light on his strategic planning, adaptability, and command over his forces. The campaign aimed to establish French control over Egypt, disrupt British trade routes, and expand French influence in the region. Despite initial military successes, the campaign faced challenges such as supply shortages and the Ottoman opposition. Napoleon's interactions with his general staff reflect his ability to navigate these obstacles and maintain cohesion within his command structure. While the campaign ultimately ended without achieving its broader objectives, its legacy includes advances in knowledge about Egypt's ancient history and culture and Napoleon's own rise as a prominent figure in European and global history.

"Napoleon and his General Staff in Egypt" by Gérôme is historically intriguing for its visual representation of Napoleon's leadership dynamics during his Egyptian campaign. Gérôme's attention to detail and vivid depiction offer a window into the challenges faced by the expedition, including the unfamiliar environment and cultural encounters. The painting becomes a visual record of Napoleon's resourcefulness and his ability to inspire his generals, reflecting the blend of military leadership, intellectual curiosity, and exploration that defined this transformative period. Through Gérôme's artistic interpretation, viewers gain a glimpse into the complexities of a campaign that both projected French power and contributed to a broader fascination with the East and its historical treasures.

Napoleon Before the Sphinx (period: 1798 - 1799) by Jean-Léon Gérôme, 1867

Napoleon Before the Sphinx

Jean-Léon Gérôme

Napoleon's encounter with the Sphinx during his 1798 Egyptian campaign remains intriguing and impactful due to its fusion of historical significance and symbolism. Amid his military conquest, Napoleon visited the ancient monument, aligning himself with the legacy of ancient conquerors while fostering his image as a modern ruler. The stark contrast between the young general and the ancient artifact highlights the ephemeral nature of human achievement against the backdrop of timeless history. This moment captures the convergence of imperial aspirations, cultural fascination, and the juxtaposition of the contemporary with the ancient, leaving an indelible mark on the historical narrative of Napoleon's ambitious endeavors.

"Napoleon Before the Sphinx" by Jean-Léon Gérôme stands as a captivating masterpiece due to its skillful interweaving of history, symbolism, and artistic technique. The painting captures a pivotal moment in time, presenting Napoleon Bonaparte, a powerful figure of his era, in contemplation before the enigmatic Great Sphinx of Giza. Gérôme's meticulous attention to historical accuracy is evident in the intricate details of Napoleon's uniform and the textured stone of the Sphinx, creating a tangible link between past and present. The composition's contrast between the modern leader and the ancient monument invites viewers to ponder the intersections of ambition, exploration, and enduring human curiosity. Through its harmonious blend of technical prowess and thought-provoking narrative, the painting serves as a window into the complexities of history and the timeless allure of ancient mysteries.

Coup of 18 Brumaire (period: 9-10 November 1799)
by Auguste Couder, 1840

Painting 10

Coup of 18 Brumaire

François Bouchot

The Coup of 18 Brumaire holds historical intrigue as a pivotal event that marked Napoleon Bonaparte's ascent to power and the transition from the tumultuous French Revolution to a more consolidated form of government. Taking place on November 9-10, 1799 (18 Brumaire in the French Republican calendar), the coup saw Napoleon, then a general, orchestrating the overthrow of the Directory, the ruling body of France. This marked the end of the revolutionary phase and led to the establishment of the Consulate, with Napoleon as First Consul. The coup highlighted Napoleon's strategic acumen, his ability to manipulate political and military forces, and the role of personal ambition in shaping historical outcomes. The event transformed France's political landscape, paving the way for Napoleon's eventual rise to becoming Emperor and reshaping the course of European history for the following decade.

"Coup of 18 Brumaire" depicted by Bouchot vividly portrays the political intrigue and military orchestration that characterized the coup, leading to the establishment of the Consulate and the consolidation of authority. Bouchot's meticulous attention to detail and emotive composition convey the tension, anticipation, and calculated moves undertaken to reshape the nation's governance. Through Bouchot's artistic lens, viewers are transported to the heart of a transformative historical event, offering insight into the blend of ambition, strategy, and historical forces that converged to redefine France's trajectory and lay the foundation for Napoleon's eventual emergence as a dominant figure in European history.

First Consul Napoleon Bonaparte (period: 1799 - 1804)
by Marie-Guillemine Benoist, 1804

Painting 11

First Consul Napoleon Bonaparte

Marie-Guillemine Benoist

Napoleon Bonaparte's role as First Consul is historically captivating due to its transformational impact on post-revolutionary France. Assuming power in 1799, Napoleon's consolidation of authority marked a pivotal shift from revolutionary turbulence to pragmatic governance. His innovative reforms modernized France's legal, educational, and administrative systems, while his charismatic leadership and military successes stabilized the nation. The Concordat with the Catholic Church and the Napoleonic Code underscored his pursuit of social cohesion and legal equality. This era showcases Napoleon's ability to balance both autocratic rule and progressive ideals, contributing to a new chapter in French history while setting the stage for his eventual imperial ascension.

Marie-Guillemine Benoist's 1804 portrait of First Consul Napoleon Bonaparte is compelling for its intimate portrayal of power and equality. Amid the backdrop of Napoleonic consolidation, the painting exudes a sense of controlled authority as Napoleon stands draped in a deep red robe, his pose evoking a blend of classical stateliness and modern command. The canvas radiates a quiet intensity, emphasizing the First Consul's measured confidence, while the restrained use of symbols and regalia imbues the portrait with a distinct contrast to more flamboyant representations of rulers. Benoist's work thus captures a pivotal juncture, where Napoleon's charismatic leadership converges with the tempered image of a nascent empire, inviting contemplation on both his transformative role and the complexities of his era.

Napoleon Crossing the Alps (period: May 1800)
by Jacques-Louis David, 1805

Painting 12

Napoleon Crossing the Alps

Jacques-Louis David

Napoleon Crossing the Alps holds fascination due to the audacity and strategic significance of the military campaign it depicts. In 1800, Napoleon led his forces through the treacherous Alpine terrain, utilizing the Great St Bernard Pass, to surprise the Austrian forces in Italy during the Second Coalition War. This daring maneuver showcased his unconventional tactics and determination, ultimately leading to the crucial Battle of Marengo. The successful crossing not only marked a turning point in the war but also solidified Napoleon's reputation as a military genius and a charismatic leader. The episode contributed to his rise as the ruler of France and left an indelible mark on European history, underlining his capacity to transform seemingly insurmountable challenges into triumphs through sheer audacity and strategic brilliance.

The painting "Napoleon Crossing the Alps" by Jacques-Louis David is a compelling masterpiece that encapsulates the grandeur and power of Napoleon Bonaparte. David's artistic prowess shines through in his portrayal of Napoleon on horseback, his commanding presence enhanced by the dramatic play of light and shadow, billowing fabric, and a mountainous backdrop. This iconic artwork not only immortalizes a pivotal moment in Napoleon's ascent to power but also captures the fusion of historical significance and artistic innovation, inviting viewers to witness the convergence of leadership, ambition, and artistic brilliance.

General Bonaparte and his Chief of Staff Berthier at the Battle of
Marengo (period: 14 June 1800) by Robert Lefevre, 1801

Painting 13

General Bonaparte and his Chief of Staff Berthier at the Battle of Marengo

Robert Lefevre

Historically, the context of "General Bonaparte and his Chief of Staff Berthier at the Battle of Marengo" is notable due to its depiction of the pivotal Battle of Marengo that occurred on June 14, 1800. As a key engagement in the War of the Second Coalition, the battle was fought between the French forces under General Napoleon Bonaparte and the Austrian army commanded by General Michael von Melas. The French initially faced setbacks but managed to turn the tide with a counterattack orchestrated by Berthier, Napoleon's chief of staff. The battle ended in a decisive French victory, solidifying Napoleon's position and influencing the subsequent Treaty of Lunéville. The battle's outcome demonstrated Napoleon's strategic acumen, his capacity to adapt to changing circumstances, and the crucial role of his subordinates in implementing successful military maneuvers. The Battle of Marengo showcased the effectiveness of Napoleon's tactics and contributed to reshaping the political and military landscape in Europe.

"General Bonaparte and his Chief of Staff Berthier at the Battle of Marengo" by Lefevre encapsulates the dynamics between Napoleon and his chief of staff, Louis-Alexandre Berthier, as they strategize on the battlefield. Through Lefevre's attention to detail and dramatic composition, viewers are immersed in the intensity of the battle and the collaborative efforts that played a decisive role in the French victory. The painting offers a glimpse into the intricacies of military command, leadership, and strategic decision-making during a pivotal engagement that solidified Napoleon's reputation as a military genius and contributed to reshaping the course of European history.

Installation of the Council of State by the First Council
(period: 1804) by Auguste Couder, 1856

Painting 14

Installation of the Council of State

Auguste Couder

Napoleon's Installation of the Council of State holds historical significance as a defining episode in his consolidation of power as Emperor of France. In 1804, Napoleon restructured the French government, establishing the Council of State as a key institution for advising and implementing policies. This event marked a crucial step in his efforts to centralize authority, streamline governance, and solidify his position as a modern ruler. The installation underscores his strategic approach to governance, blending the traditions of monarchy with the changing landscape of post-revolutionary France. It reflects his ambition to create a stable and efficient administration, while also shaping the trajectory of the country's political and administrative framework during his reign.

"Installation of the Council of State" by Auguste Couder is historically intriguing as it captures a seminal moment in Napoleon Bonaparte's imperial reign. Painted in 1837, the artwork depicts Napoleon addressing the newly formed Council of State in 1804, reflecting his consolidation of authority and innovative governance. Couder's composition emphasizes the Emperor's commanding presence and the attentive assembly of dignitaries, embodying Napoleon's vision of centralized power while echoing the historical grandeur of earlier monarchs. The painting encapsulates Napoleon's multifaceted approach to leadership, melding tradition with his modern administrative strategies, offering a vivid snapshot of his lasting impact on the reshaping of France's political landscape.

The Coronation of Napoleon (period: 2 December 1804) by Jacques-Louis David, 1807

Painting 15

The Coronation of Napoleon

Jacques-Louis David

The Coronation of Napoleon stands as a pivotal historical spectacle that encapsulates Napoleon Bonaparte's ingenious blend of tradition and innovation. In 1804, at Notre Dame Cathedral in Paris, Napoleon orchestrated a grand ceremony where he crowned himself Emperor of the French, symbolizing the continuity of monarchy while redefining power dynamics. By taking the crown from the Pope's hands and placing it on his own head, Napoleon demonstrated his supremacy over both church and state. This audacious act reflected his ability to leverage symbols and rituals to consolidate authority, while simultaneously signaling his break from the revolutionary ideals that had previously defined French governance. The event showcased Napoleon's adeptness at shaping his image as a ruler, straddling the line between ancient monarchies and a modern imperial era, and leaving an indelible mark on the course of European history.

"The Coronation of Napoleon" by Jacques-Louis David holds historical fascination as a masterful depiction of a transformative event in European history. The artwork immortalizes Napoleon Bonaparte's crowning as Emperor of the French in 1804, showcasing the intricate interplay of tradition and innovation. David's meticulous attention to detail and composition captures the opulence and pageantry of the ceremony at Notre Dame Cathedral, while his deliberate inclusion of historical figures, gestures, and symbols reinforces Napoleon's imperial legitimacy. The painting serves as both a visual testament to Napoleon's mastery of spectacle and a reflection of his ability to wield art for political propaganda, cementing his legacy as a towering figure who reshaped the course of France and Europe during the Napoleonic era.

Napoleon in Coronation Robes (period: 2 December 1804)
by Anne-Louis Girodet de Roussy-Trioson, 1812

Painting 16

Napoleon in Coronation Robes

Anne-Louis Girodet de Roussy-Trioson

In the lesser-known context of Napoleon in coronation robes, it's intriguing to note that his choice of attire for his coronation as Emperor of the French in 1804 was heavily influenced by his desire to fuse symbolism from both the ancient Roman Empire and the medieval Carolingian dynasty. While the overall grandeur of his coronation attire is well-documented, lesser-known is the inclusion of elements that sought to establish his imperial legitimacy by drawing connections to historical precedents. The use of bees as a decorative motif, for instance, harked back to the Merovingian kings, while the Roman-style toga and laurel wreath he wore signaled his identification with the Caesars. This amalgamation of historical references in his attire aimed to project a continuity of authority while asserting his imperial position in a unique and compelling manner.

"Napoleon in Coronation Robes" by Anne-Louis Girodet de Roussy-Trioson is historically intriguing for its portrayal of Napoleon Bonaparte's complex relationship with power, authority, and self-presentation. Created in 1812, the artwork captures Napoleon dressed in regal coronation robes, reflecting his transformation from a military general to Emperor of the French. Girodet's meticulous attention to detail and emotive composition convey the blend of majesty and vulnerability in Napoleon's posture and expression. The painting delves into the psychological intricacies of a leader who sought to project an image of imperial grandeur while also grappling with the implications of his role. It offers a nuanced insight into the interplay between personal identity, political ambition, and the performative nature of authority, providing viewers with a glimpse into the complexities of Napoleon's reign and the intricate narratives of power and self-representation that defined his era.

Napoleon on His Imperial Throne (period: 1804)
by Jean-Auguste-Dominique Ingres, 1806

Painting 17

Napoleon on His Imperial Throne

Jean-Auguste-Dominique Ingres

Historically, Napoleon on his imperial throne reflects a pivotal juncture in Napoleon Bonaparte's ascent to absolute power as Emperor of the French in 1804. This transformation from a revolutionary general to an imperial ruler marked a significant shift in the political landscape of France and Europe. By crowning himself Emperor, Napoleon sought to consolidate his authority and establish a stable government after years of revolutionary turmoil. The coronation ceremony at Notre Dame Cathedral showcased his strategic blend of historical symbolism and contemporary spectacle, reinforcing his image as a legitimate and powerful ruler. This moment underscores his ability to manipulate and adapt historical traditions to serve his ambitions.

"Napoleon on His Imperial Throne," painted by Jean-Auguste-Dominique Ingres in 1806, holds historical fascination due to its strategic portrayal of Napoleon Bonaparte's imperial authority. The painting captures the Emperor seated on an ornate throne, adorned in rich regalia, emanating a sense of majestic power. Ingres's meticulous attention to detail, from the intricate patterns of the upholstery to the intricate decorations, underscores Napoleon's deliberate cultivation of a new imperial aesthetic. This work encapsulates the emperor's skilled manipulation of artistic representation to solidify his legitimacy and project an aura of opulence and authority. The painting not only serves as a testament to Napoleon's mastery of propaganda but also provides a visual snapshot of his grand ambitions during the zenith of his rule, contributing to the enduring mythos surrounding his imperial reign.

Napoleon Reviewing the Guard in the Place du Carrousel (period: 1804 - 1814) by Horace Vernet, 1836

Painting 18

Napoleon Reviewing the Guard in the Place du Carrousel

Horace Vernet

Napoleon reviewing the guard in the place du Carrousel captures a symbolic moment of Napoleon Bonaparte's consolidation of power and his relationship with the military. The event, which took place in 1804, showcased Napoleon's ability to command loyalty and admiration from his troops while reinforcing his image as a strong and charismatic leader. The review displayed the meticulous organization and grandeur of his military displays, serving to solidify his authority and influence. This event marked a pivotal juncture in Napoleon's trajectory, as he transitioned from First Consul to Emperor of the French. The review underscored the potency of his charisma, the aura of his leadership, and the blend of military might and political acumen that defined his reign.

"Napoleon Reviewing the Guard in the Place du Carrousel" by Vernet is historically captivating for its depiction of a ceremonial moment that encapsulates Napoleon's mastery of image and power. The painting immortalizes the event of Napoleon's review of his Imperial Guard in 1810, emphasizing the symbiotic relationship between the ruler and his military forces. Vernet's attention to detail and dynamic composition capture the grandeur of the occasion, highlighting the precision of the troops' formations and the aura of authority that surrounded Napoleon. Through his skillful brushwork, Vernet brings to life the grandiosity and calculated theatrics of Napoleon's rule, showcasing his ability to cultivate a magnetic presence and project a sense of invincibility. The painting underscores the interplay of charisma, spectacle, and leadership that characterized Napoleon's reign, offering a glimpse into the fascinating interplay of personality and politics during this transformative era.

Emperor Napoleon in His Study at the Tuileries
(period: 1804 - 1815) by Jacques-Louis David, 1812

Painting 19

Emperor Napoleon in His Study
at the Tuileries

Jacques-Louis David

Napoleon in his study at the Tuileries presents a captivating historical tableau that encapsulates the essence of his rule. The scene conveys a potent mix of power and introspection as the Emperor engages in administrative and strategic contemplation within the heart of his regime. This intimate glimpse into Napoleon's private sphere symbolizes his meticulous attention to governance, showcasing his multifaceted persona as a military genius, statesman, and visionary leader. The study serves as a microcosm of his empire, where his ambition and intellect intersect, leaving an enduring impression of his complex character and the indelible mark he left on France and European history.

"Emperor Napoleon in His Study at the Tuileries" by Jacques-Louis David is remarkable for its portrayal of Napoleon Bonaparte's commanding presence amid an intimate setting, capturing the essence of his rule. The painting reveals Napoleon deep in contemplation within his study, surrounded by symbols of power and intellect. His focused expression and regal demeanor reflect his multifaceted role as both a military leader and a statesman, while the opulent decor and historical artifacts emphasize his authority. The artwork encapsulates Napoleon's mastery of propaganda and self-presentation, offering a glimpse into the calculated image he projected to reinforce his imperial status. Through the seamless fusion of personal and political narratives, David's painting becomes a lasting testament to Napoleon's lasting influence and complex legacy in European history.

The Distribution of the Eagle Standards (period: 5 December 1804) by Jacques-Louis David, 1810

Painting 20

The Distribution of the Eagle Standards

Jacques-Louis David

The Distribution of the Eagle Standards holds historical significance as a ceremonial event that marked a pivotal moment during Napoleon's reign. Taking place in 1804, it was part of the Napoleonic strategy to strengthen his political legitimacy and rally the loyalty of his military forces. The distribution of the newly designed imperial eagle standards to various regiments symbolized a unifying connection between the French army and the regime, highlighting the shift from the revolutionary fervor to a more consolidated and centralized authority under Napoleon's rule. This event reinforced the military's allegiance to the emperor, solidified his position as the head of state, and reflected his mastery in harnessing symbolism for political purposes. The eagle standards represented not only military valor but also a fusion of nationalism and loyalty to Napoleon's vision, showcasing the blend of military, political, and symbolic elements that characterized his rule.

"The Distribution of the Eagle Standards" by David vividly captures the ceremonial event in which Napoleon distributed new imperial eagle standards to his troops, cementing their loyalty and emphasizing his authority. Through David's meticulous attention to detail and dramatic composition, viewers are transported to a juncture where symbolism, military power, and political messaging converged. The painting reflects Napoleon's mastery in using art to bolster his image and political agenda, showcasing his ability to leverage symbolism to unite his forces and establish his legitimacy as a leader. It offers a glimpse into the calculated theatricality that characterized Napoleon's rule and how visual representation played a crucial role in shaping perceptions of power and loyalty.

The Battle of Austerlitz (period: 2 December 1805) by Gérard François, 1808

Painting 21

The Battle of Austerlitz

Gérard François

The Battle of Austerlitz, fought on December 2, 1805, is historically remarkable for its strategic brilliance and profound impact on the Napoleonic Wars. Also known as the "Battle of the Three Emperors," it pitted Napoleon Bonaparte's French forces against the Russian and Austrian armies. Napoleon's innovative tactics and careful orchestration of his troops resulted in a decisive victory for the French, showcasing his unparalleled military genius. The battle's outcome led to the signing of the Treaty of Pressburg, securing major territorial gains for France and weakening the Third Coalition against Napoleon. Austerlitz is regarded as one of Napoleon's greatest triumphs, highlighting his ability to exploit terrain, anticipate his opponents' moves, and execute complex maneuvers. The battle altered the balance of power in Europe, consolidating Napoleon's authority and reshaping the continent's political landscape.

"The Battle of Austerlitz" by François vividly captures the intensity, tactics, and strategic brilliance of the battle. François's attention to detail and dramatic composition convey the chaos, valor, and calculated maneuvers that marked Napoleon Bonaparte's triumphant victory against the Russian and Austrian armies. Through François's artistic interpretation, viewers are transported to the heart of the battle, offering a glimpse into the ferocity of combat and the pivotal role of leadership and strategy in shaping the course of world events. The painting becomes a visual portal to an epochal clash that redefined European geopolitics, highlighting the convergence of military prowess, innovation, and historical significance.

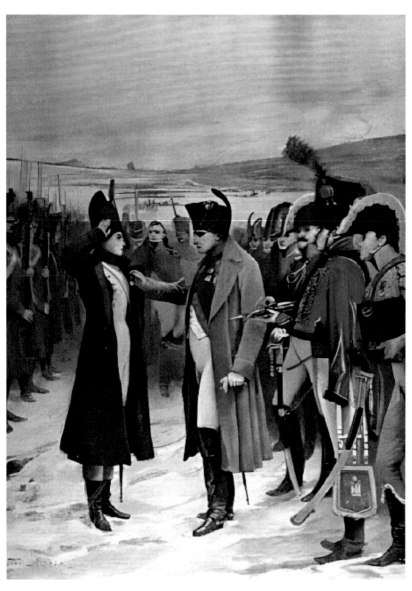

Napoleon Presenting Marie Schellinck a Medal on the Battlefield
(period: 1805) by Lionel Noël Royer, 1894

Painting 22

Napoleon Presenting Marie Schellinck a Medal on the Battlefield

Lionel Noël Royer

Napoleon presenting Marie Schellinck, a female officer, with a medal on the battlefield stands as a vivid testament to the unconventional intersections of gender, bravery, and military recognition in an era dominated by traditional gender norms. At a time when women's roles in combat and leadership were limited, Schellinck's acknowledgment by no less than Napoleon himself was not just a personal tribute to her valor, but a broader acknowledgment that courage and competence in the field of battle were not the exclusive purview of men. This event was a striking deviation from the era's prevailing norms and, in its own way, challenged established notions of gender and heroism, making it an indelible moment in the annals of military history.

Lionel Noël Royer's depiction of Napoleon presenting a medal to Marie Schellinck on the battlefield is a powerful artistic representation that resonates beyond its immediate subject matter. Through Royer's brush, this moment transcends mere historical record, emerging as a stirring tableau of defiance against societal norms. By immortalizing Schellinck's bravery and Napoleon's acknowledgment of it, Royer captures a unique intersection of gender, heroism, and military honor in the Napoleonic era. The artwork serves as a visual testament to the potential for individuals, irrespective of gender, to rise to the heights of valor, and the capacity for great leaders to recognize and celebrate such acts of courage. It's a compelling reminder that heroism knows no gender, and art, at its best, can challenge and reshape societal narratives.

The Battle of Jena (period: 14 October 1806) by Horace Vernet, 1836

Painting 23

Battle of Jena

Horace Vernet

The Battle of Jena, fought in 1806 during the War of the Fourth Coalition, is historically captivating for its transformative impact on European politics and military strategy. The battle pitted Napoleon Bonaparte's French forces against the Prussian army led by Frederick William III. Napoleon's brilliant implementation of the maneuver known as the "double envelopment" led to a decisive victory, showcasing his innovative tactics and the effectiveness of his Grande Armée. The defeat of the Prussian forces marked a turning point in the Napoleonic Wars, reshaping the power dynamics across Europe and highlighting the prowess of Napoleon's military strategy. The battle's outcome underscored the supremacy of modernized warfare and positioned Napoleon as a dominant figure on the European stage, solidifying his reputation as a military genius and advancing his ambitions to reshape the continent's political order.

"Battle of Jena" by Horace Vernet is historically captivating for its vivid portrayal of the pivotal 1806 battle during the Napoleonic Wars. Created in 1836, the painting captures the intensity and chaos of the clash between Napoleon's French forces and the Prussian army. Vernet's meticulous attention to detail and dynamic composition convey the scale of the conflict, the interplay of cavalry charges and infantry formations, and the fervor of battle. Through his skillful brushwork, Vernet brings to life the raw emotions, struggles, and sacrifices endured by soldiers on both sides. The artwork not only serves as a visual record of the battle's intricacies but also offers insight into the brutal realities of warfare during the era, encapsulating the broader narrative of Napoleon's dominance and the changing contours of European geopolitics.

Napoleon on the Battlefield of Eylau (period: 7-8 February 1807) by Antoine-Jean Gros, 1808

Painting 24

Napoleon on the Battlefield of Eylau

Antoine-Jean Gros

The historical significance of Napoleon on the Battlefield of Eylau lies in its portrayal of a critical moment during the Napoleonic Wars, reflecting both Napoleon Bonaparte's military prowess and the brutality of warfare. The Battle of Eylau in 1807 was a pivotal clash between Napoleon's French forces and the Russian Empire, marked by its staggering casualties and ferocity. Napoleon's decision to stay on the battlefield despite the harsh winter conditions demonstrated his strategic acumen and hands-on leadership style, while the intense fighting and heavy losses underscored the grim realities of war. This engagement, depicted in the painting, serves as a microcosm of the broader Napoleonic conflicts, highlighting the era's violent struggles for dominance and Napoleon's role as a strategic genius capable of both triumph and sacrifice in pursuit of his grand ambitions.

"Napoleon on the Battlefield of Eylau" by Antoine-Jean Gros carries historical intrigue as a vivid representation of a pivotal moment in the Napoleonic Wars. Painted in 1808, the artwork captures Napoleon Bonaparte's presence at the Battle of Eylau in 1807, a clash marked by its intense brutality and strategic significance. Gros's portrayal of Napoleon amidst the aftermath of the battle conveys the stark realities of war, emphasizing both his resilience and the human cost of his ambitions. The painting encapsulates the harsh conditions, profound challenges, and personal stakes of the Napoleonic conflicts, offering a poignant snapshot of Napoleon's leadership style and the complex emotions of warfare during this transformative era in European history.

Napoleon at the Battlefield of Friedland (period: 14 June 1807)
by Horace Vernet, 1835

Painting 25

Napoleon at the
Battle of Friedland

Horace Vernet

Napoleon at the battle of Friedland is historically compelling as it represents a pivotal moment during the Napoleonic Wars. Fought in 1807 between Napoleon's French forces and the Russian Empire, the battle showcased Napoleon's strategic brilliance and innovative tactics. His deft maneuvering led to a decisive victory that solidified his dominance in Europe and compelled Russia to seek peace. The battle underscored Napoleon's adeptness at exploiting terrain and orchestrating complex military maneuvers, positioning him as a formidable military strategist. The resulting Treaty of Tilsit reshaped European geopolitics, fostering a brief period of détente between France and Russia. Napoleon's triumph at Friedland marked a high point in his military career, further solidifying his reputation as a masterful commander and exerting a profound influence on the trajectory of European history during the early 19th century.

"Napoleon at the Battle of Friedland" by Vernet is historically captivating for its visual representation of a decisive moment during the Napoleonic Wars. The painting immortalizes Napoleon Bonaparte's leadership during the Battle of Friedland in 1807. Vernet's attention to detail and dynamic composition capture the intensity of the conflict, emphasizing Napoleon's charismatic presence on the battlefield and his strategic acumen. The artwork becomes a visual testimony to the convergence of military prowess, leadership, and the transformational impact of Napoleon's strategies. Through Vernet's brushwork, viewers gain insight into the complexities of warfare and the larger narrative of Napoleon's rise as a military genius, offering a glimpse into the interconnectedness of individual brilliance and historical shifts that marked this pivotal era.

Napoleon at the Gates of Madrid (period: December 1808) by Antoine-Jean Gros, 1808

Painting 26

Napoleon at the Gates of Madrid

Antoine-Jean Gros

"Napoleon at the Gates of Madrid" carries historical significance as it symbolizes a critical moment during the Peninsular War. In December 1808, Napoleon Bonaparte personally led French forces in an attempt to capture Madrid, a strategic move to secure control over Spain. This event underscores the challenges faced by Napoleon's armies in the Peninsular War, characterized by guerrilla resistance and popular uprisings against French occupation. The historical event marked both Napoleon's attempt to assert dominance over Spain and the Spanish people's fierce resistance to foreign occupation, contributing to the protracted and complex nature of the Peninsular War, a conflict that left a profound impact on the course of European history.

"Napoleon at the Gates of Madrid" by Antoine-Jean Gros is historically captivating for its depiction of a critical juncture during the Peninsular War. Painted in 1808, the artwork vividly portrays Napoleon Bonaparte's commanding presence at the siege of Madrid, reflecting his ambition to assert French dominance in Spain. Gros's dynamic composition captures the intensity of the conflict and the formidable figure of Napoleon amidst the chaos of battle. This painting offers a visual narrative of the complex interplay between military strategy, political maneuvering, and the persistent resistance of local populations, providing a potent glimpse into the turbulent Peninsular War and the far-reaching ramifications of Napoleonic expansion across Europe.

The Battle of Wagram (period: 5-6 July 1809) by Horace Vernet, 1836

Painting 27

Battle of Wagram

Horace Vernet

The Battle of Wagram, fought between the French Empire and the Austrian Empire in July 1809, holds historical significance as one of the largest and bloodiest conflicts during the Napoleonic Wars. This engagement marked Napoleon Bonaparte's attempt to secure his influence over Central Europe and quell Austrian opposition. The prolonged battle demonstrated the scale of Napoleonic warfare, with hundreds of thousands of troops engaged in intense combat over several days. The Austrian forces presented a formidable challenge, forcing Napoleon to adapt his strategies. Ultimately, Napoleon's tactical brilliance secured a French victory, but the high casualty rates on both sides highlighted the human cost of his ambitious expansionist campaigns. The Battle of Wagram contributed to the reshaping of European power dynamics, underscored the resilience of Austrian resistance, and revealed both the might and limitations of Napoleon's military might during this transformative era.

"Battle of Wagram" by Vernet is historically captivating for its vivid portrayal of a pivotal moment during the Napoleonic Wars. Vernet's meticulous attention to detail and dynamic composition convey the scale of the conflict and the dramatic interplay between cavalry charges, infantry formations, and artillery fire. The painting not only showcases Vernet's masterful technique but also offers a visual narrative of the raw emotions, struggles, and sacrifices endured by soldiers on both sides. The Battle of Wagram, a critical juncture in European history, becomes tangible through Vernet's skillful brushwork, providing a gripping testament to the brutality and complexity of Napoleonic warfare and its profound impact on the course of continental geopolitics.

Napoleon's Farewell to Josephine (period: 15 December 1809)
by Lionel Noël Royer, 1835

Painting 28

Napoleon's Farewell to Josephine

Lionel Noël Royer

Napoleon's Farewell to Josephine stands as a pivotal moment in the annals of European history, underscoring the tension between personal affection and political exigency. Their relationship, once the toast of Paris, was marked by both deep passion and tumult. Yet, as the ruler of a vast empire, Napoleon was acutely aware of the need for a direct heir to ensure its continuity. The fact that Josephine, despite their bond, could not provide him with an heir led to their painful separation. Historically, this event highlights the stark choices faced by rulers, where the demands of the state can often override personal desires. Napoleon's decision to annul his marriage to Josephine in favor of establishing a more secure lineage underscores the sacrifices demanded by power and the intricate interplay between personal and political imperatives in the lives of historic figures.

Lionel Noël Royer's painting "Napoleon's Farewell to Josephine" captures a poignant intersection of personal emotion and political necessity in European history. Royer's portrayal of this heart-wrenching moment, when Napoleon chooses statecraft over personal affection, vividly encapsulates the tension faced by leaders when private desires clash with public duty. In the artwork, the raw emotion on Napoleon and Josephine's faces serves as a powerful testament to their genuine love, even as the demands of empire force them apart. Historically interesting and impressionable, the painting offers viewers a glimpse into the sacrifices demanded by leadership and the heartache that can lurk behind monumental political decisions. Through Royer's brushstrokes, a deeply personal moment in Napoleon's life becomes emblematic of the perennial conflict between love and duty.

On the Eve of the Battle of Borodino (period: 6 September 1812) by Horace Vernet, 1836

Painting 29

On the Eve of the
Battle of Borodino

Horace Vernet

On the eve of the battle of Borodino is historically compelling
as it captures the anticipation and gravity of a crucial moment
during Napoleon's ill-fated invasion of Russia in 1812. The painting
metaphorically represents the profound sense of impending conflict
and the somber reflection that often precedes pivotal engagements.
The Battle of Borodino marked a culmination of strategic maneuvers
and political tensions, with both French and Russian forces heavily
invested in the outcome. The event holds significance not only for
its impact on the Napoleonic Wars but also for its portrayal of the
immense human cost and the broader complexities of empire-
building and military expansion. The painting's title encapsulates
the dramatic convergence of political ambition, military strategy,
and individual choices that shaped this pivotal period in European
history.

"On the Eve of the Battle of Borodino" by Horace Vernet is
historically fascinating for its visual encapsulation of the intense
emotions and charged atmosphere preceding the Battle of Borodino
in 1812. Crafted in 1836, the painting vividly captures the grim
anticipation and camaraderie among Napoleon Bonaparte's
soldiers on the cusp of a decisive clash with Russian forces. Vernet's
meticulous attention to detail and emotive composition convey the
gravity of the situation, depicting a mix of determination, trepidation,
and unity among the troops. Through Vernet's brushstrokes, viewers
are transported to the tense moment before a significant battle,
offering a glimpse into the human experience and the emotional
undercurrents that define the pivotal events of history.

Napoleon at the Battle of Borodino (period: 7 September 1812) by Louis-François Lejeune, 1822

Painting 30

Napoleon at the
Battle of Borodino

Louis-François Lejeune

Napoleon at the Battle of Borodino in 1812 holds historical fascination due to its position as a defining engagement during Napoleon's ill-fated invasion of Russia. Fought during the Napoleonic Wars, the battle saw Napoleon's Grande Armée clashing with Russian forces in a brutal conflict marked by staggering casualties. The battle's significance lies in its portrayal of the tremendous human cost and strategic complexities of Napoleon's ambitions. The inability to secure a decisive victory highlighted the daunting challenges of conducting a vast campaign in harsh Russian terrain. The high toll on both sides and the destructive aftermath marked a turning point in Napoleon's power and set the stage for his eventual downfall. The Battle of Borodino encapsulates the confluence of military strategy, political ambition, and the grim realities of warfare, reflecting the complex interplay between individual leaders and the unfolding course of history.

Napoleon at the Battle of Borodino depicted by Lejeune captures the intensity and chaos of the battle, revealing the strategic complexity and human toll of the conflict. Lejeune's attention to detail and emotive composition convey the relentless fighting and the commanding presence of Napoleon on the field. Through Lejeune's brushwork, viewers gain a visceral sense of the harsh realities faced by both French and Russian forces, reflecting the convergence of military strategy, attrition, and the dire consequences of Napoleon's ambitious expansion. The painting becomes a visual record of a pivotal moment in history, offering insight into the dynamics of warfare, leadership, and the lasting impact of monumental campaigns on the course of world events.

Napoleon on the Borodino Heights (period: 7 September 1812) by Vasily Vereshchagin, 1897

Painting 31

Napoleon on the Borodino Heights

Vasily Vereshchagin

Napoleon on the Borodino heights is historically intriguing due
to its portrayal of a pivotal moment during Napoleon Bonaparte's
ill-fated Russian campaign in 1812. As he surveyed the battlefield
from the heights after the Battle of Borodino, Napoleon confronted
the harsh realities of his expedition: dwindling forces, casualties, and
the relentless Russian resistance. This event marked a turning point
in the campaign, revealing the challenges posed by the vast Russian
terrain, brutal weather, and tenacious enemy forces. The aftermath of
Borodino set the stage for the subsequent retreat and the unraveling
of Napoleon's once-mighty empire, underlining the significance of
this juncture in the larger context of his military endeavors and the
course of European history.

"Napoleon on the Borodino Heights" by Vasily Vereshchagin is
historically captivating for its depiction of a pivotal moment during
the French invasion of Russia in 1812. Painted in 1897, the artwork
portrays Napoleon Bonaparte as he surveys the battlefield after the
Battle of Borodino, showcasing the aftermath of the intense conflict.
Vereshchagin's attention to detail and atmospheric depiction capture
the solemn atmosphere and the devastation that marked this critical
juncture of the campaign. The painting's somber tones and careful
rendering evoke the harsh realities faced by both sides, emphasizing
the human toll and the harshness of warfare. As a witness to history,
Vereshchagin's portrayal adds depth to the understanding of
Napoleon's ill-fated expedition, inviting viewers to contemplate the
impact of hubris, geopolitics, and the stark consequences of military
pursuits on a grand scale.

In Gorodnya - To Breakthrough or Retreat? (period: 1812) by Vasily Vereshchagin, 1896

Painting 32

In Gorodnya -
To Breakthrough or Retreat?

Vasily Vereshchagin

"In Gorodnya - To Breakthrough or Retreat?" holds historical
significance for its representation of a critical juncture during the
Battle of Krasnoi in 1812, a pivotal episode in Napoleon's disastrous
Russian campaign. As French forces faced encirclement by Russian
armies, the question of whether to push forward or retreat became a
fateful decision. The battle showcases the dire predicament faced by
Napoleon's Grande Armée in the harsh Russian winter. The outcome
at Krasnoi symbolizes the harrowing challenges of maintaining a
massive invasion force far from home, the resilience of Russian
resistance, and the human toll exacted by the campaign. The event
underscores the complexities of military strategy, logistics, and
the brutal realities of warfare in unforgiving conditions. The Battle
of Krasnoi marked a turning point in the campaign's fortunes,
ultimately contributing to Napoleon's decline and reshaping the
trajectory of European history.

"In Gorodnya - To Breakthrough or Retreat" by Vereshchagin
captures the tension and desperation as French soldiers confront the
dilemma of either pushing forward to break through Russian lines
or retreating in the face of encirclement. Vereshchagin's attention to
detail and emotional composition convey the gravity of the situation,
depicting the physical and emotional toll exacted by a brutal
campaign. Through Vereshchagin's artistic perspective, viewers are
transported to the heart of a critical juncture in Napoleon's Russian
campaign, offering a glimpse into the agonizing decisions, human
endurance, and the complex interplay between individual actions
and the unfolding course of history.

Eugène de Beauharnais and Napoleon in Russia (period: 1812) by Adam Albrecht, 1835

Painting 33

Eugène de Beauharnais and Napoleon in Russia

Adam Albrecht

"Eugène de Beauharnais and Napoleon in Russia" holds historical interest as it sheds light on the significant role played by Napoleon Bonaparte's stepson, Eugène de Beauharnais, during the challenging Russian campaign of 1812. Eugène, serving as Napoleon's Viceroy of Italy, was entrusted with military and diplomatic responsibilities that showcased his capabilities as a leader. The campaign itself marked a pivotal juncture in their relationship, as they navigated the complexities of a harsh Russian winter and the formidable resistance of Russian forces. The historical context underscores the multifaceted nature of familial and political dynamics within Napoleon's inner circle, providing insights into the strategic decisions and personal interactions that shaped their roles in this critical period.

"Eugène de Beauharnais and Napoleon in Russia" by Adam Albrecht is historically intriguing for its visual portrayal of the bond between Napoleon and his stepson Eugène de Beauharnais during the challenging Russian campaign. The artwork captures the dynamics of their relationship amidst the demanding circumstances of warfare and diplomacy. Albrecht's attention to detail and emotive composition convey the complexities of familial and political ties as they navigated the hardships of the campaign. Through the painting, viewers gain insight into the collaborative efforts, strategic decision-making, and personal dynamics that shaped their roles in a pivotal chapter of European history. The artwork becomes a visual gateway to the intricacies of leadership, loyalty, and familial connections against the backdrop of a transformative historical event.

Napoleon's Retreat from Russia (period: 1812) by Vasily Vereshchagin, 1851

Painting 34

Napoleon's Retreat from Russia

Adolph Northen

Napoleon's retreat from Russia in 1812 stands as a poignant and consequential chapter in his military campaigns. Following his ill-fated invasion of Russia with the largest army Europe had ever seen, Napoleon's forces suffered catastrophic losses due to the harsh Russian winter, dwindling supplies, and fierce Russian resistance. The retreat marked a humbling turning point in his ambitions, resulting in the near-collapse of his once-mighty empire. This event showcased the perils of overextension and the stark realities of warfare, reshaping the European balance of power and marking the beginning of the end for Napoleon's dominance. The retreat from Russia became emblematic of the hubris and challenges that shaped his downfall, offering a poignant lesson on the complexities of military strategy, the consequences of geopolitical ambitions, and the endurance of historical memory.

"Napoleon's Retreat from Russia" by Adolph Northen is historically striking for its portrayal of a pivotal and tragic episode in Napoleon Bonaparte's military career. Northen's attention to detail and emotive depiction of the retreating soldiers and the desolate winter landscape conveys the stark reality of the disastrous expedition. The painting provides a visual testimony to the sheer magnitude of suffering, mortality, and desolation endured by Napoleon's forces during their retreat from Russia. By portraying this traumatic event, Northen's work underscores the human cost and profound impact of Napoleon's ambitions, and serves as a testament to the resilience of historical memory, echoing the somber lessons of hubris and the complexities of military endeavors on a grand scale.

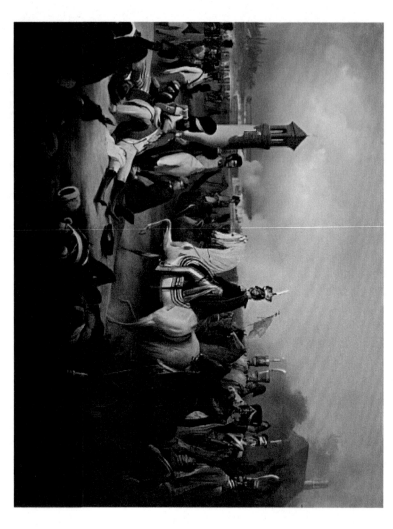

Napoleon's Retreat from Russia (period: 16-19 October 1813) by Vasily Vereshchagin, ~1850

Painting 35

Battle of Leipzig

January Suchodolski

The Battle of Leipzig, also known as the Battle of Nations, is historically compelling as one of the largest and bloodiest conflicts of the Napoleonic Wars during October 1813. The battle pitted Napoleon's French forces against a coalition of European powers including Austria, Prussia, Russia, and Sweden. The outcome of the battle marked a significant turning point in Napoleon's fortunes, as his defeat signaled the weakening of his grip over Europe. The victory of the coalition forces led to the eventual downfall of Napoleon's empire, highlighting the strength of collective resistance against his expansionist ambitions and reshaping the political map of Europe. The Battle of Leipzig thus emerges as a monumental event that underscored the challenges and complexities of Napoleonic warfare, and played a crucial role in the trajectory of European history during this transformative era.

"Battle of Leipzig" by Suchodolski vividly captures the intensity and chaos of the battle as Napoleon's French forces clashed with the coalition armies of European nations. Suchodolski's meticulous attention to detail and dynamic composition convey the scale of the conflict, the interplay of various military units, and the emotional charge of warfare. Through his masterful brushwork, he brings to life the intricate strategies, sacrifices, and challenges faced by soldiers on both sides. The painting not only serves as a visual record of the battle's intricacies but also offers a glimpse into the tumultuous events that shaped the course of European history, reflecting the grandeur and devastation of Napoleonic warfare on a monumental scale.

Bidding Farewell to the Imperial Guard at Fontainebleau (period: April 1814) by Horace Vernet, 1826

Painting 36

Bidding Farewell to the Imperial Guard at Fontainebleau

Horace Vernet

"Bidding Farewell to the Imperial Guard at Fontainebleau" holds historical significance as a poignant testament to the downfall of Napoleon Bonaparte's empire. In 1814, after a series of military defeats and political pressures, Napoleon abdicated the throne and was exiled to the island of Elba. The depicted scene, set in Fontainebleau Palace, captures the heart-wrenching moment when Napoleon bid farewell to his loyal Imperial Guard, soldiers who had fiercely supported him throughout his campaigns. This event encapsulates the human aspect of power's decline, as Napoleon faced the consequences of his ambitions and the dissolution of his once-mighty rule. The painting reflects the dramatic shift in European geopolitics and the eventual trajectory towards Napoleon's brief return to power in the Hundred Days, followed by his final exile to Saint Helena, culminating in the definitive end of his imperial reign and marking a significant chapter in the history of the Napoleonic era.

"Bidding Farewell to the Imperial Guard at Fontainebleau" by Horace Vernet, holds historical resonance as a poignant depiction of the culmination of Napoleon Bonaparte's dramatic rise and fall. Vernet's composition humanizes the grand narrative of power, portraying the Emperor as a figure of vulnerability and reflection amidst the dedicated soldiers who had stood by his side. The artwork encapsulates the emotional and geopolitical complexity of this turning point in European history, where the once-mighty ruler faced the consequences of his ambitions and marked the end of his remarkable era, offering a lasting visual testament to the intersection of personal drama and historical transition.

Napoleon at Fontainebleau (period: April 1814)
by Paul Delaroche, 1840

Painting 37

Napoleon at Fontainebleau

Paul Delaroche

Napoleon at Fontainebleau holds historical significance as it captures a poignant chapter in Napoleon Bonaparte's life and the end of his rule. In 1814, after a series of military setbacks and political pressures, Napoleon abdicated the throne and was exiled to the island of Elba. His departure from Fontainebleau marked his relinquishment of power and the changing tides of European politics. This event signaled the conclusion of his domination over France and Europe, reflecting the culmination of his ambitious rise and eventual fall. The departure from Fontainebleau foreshadowed his eventual return and the dramatic "Hundred Days," leading to his final exile to Saint Helena, which marked the definitive end of his rule and the conclusion of an era that had profoundly reshaped the course of European history.

"Napoleon at Fontainebleau" by Paul Delaroche is historically evocative for its portrayal of a pivotal moment in Napoleon Bonaparte's life. Delaroche's meticulous attention to detail and emotional resonance convey the weight of the moment as Napoleon faces the end of his rule. The painting encapsulates the vulnerability and contemplation of a once-mighty leader at a crossroads, inviting viewers to reflect on the complexities of power, ambition, and the inevitability of historical transitions. By immortalizing this crucial juncture, Delaroche's work resonates with the broader historical narrative of Napoleon's rise and fall, offering a poignant insight into the human dimension of leadership and the passage of an era.

Napoleon Leaving the Island of Elba (period: 26 February 1815) by Joseph Beaume, 1836

Painting 38

Napoleon Leaving the
Island of Elba

Joseph Beaume

The historical event of Napoleon Bonaparte leaving the island of
Elba in 1815 is deeply intriguing as it marked his audacious return
to power after his initial abdication and exile. Escaping Elba and
re-entering France, Napoleon embarked on what became known as
the "Hundred Days," a brief but dramatic episode of his attempted
resurgence. His return ignited a flurry of political and military
activity, challenging the stability that had been established after his
initial downfall. This audacious move intensified the already complex
European political landscape, leading to his subsequent defeat at
the Battle of Waterloo and final exile to Saint Helena. The event
underscores Napoleon's indomitable spirit, the enduring allure of his
leadership, and the profound impact of his presence on the course of
modern European history.

The portrayal of "Napoleon Leaving the Island of Elba" by Joseph
Beaume holds historical intrigue as it captures a pivotal moment in
Napoleon's life. Created in 1836, the artwork visualizes Napoleon's
departure from exile on the island of Elba in 1815, marking his
audacious return to the European stage. Beaume's representation
conveys the gravity of the event, highlighting the decisive shift in
the political landscape and the subsequent "Hundred Days." The
painting becomes a visual testament to Napoleon's determination,
challenging the status quo and setting in motion a sequence of events
that would reshape the trajectory of European politics and warfare.
Through Beaume's skillful rendering, viewers are offered a glimpse
into the audacity and impact of a historical figure whose actions
continued to reverberate long after his exile began.

Napoleon at Waterloo (period: 18 June 1815)
by Ernest Meissonier, 1862

Napoleon at Waterloo

Ernest Meissonier

Napoleon at Waterloo holds profound historical significance as it marks the culmination of Napoleon's tumultuous career and his ultimate defeat. The Battle of Waterloo, fought on June 18, 1815, near present-day Belgium, witnessed the clash between Napoleon's forces and a coalition of British, Prussian, and allied troops. Napoleon's ambitions for a triumphant return to power were dashed by his adversaries' coordinated efforts, ultimately resulting in his decisive defeat and subsequent exile to Saint Helena. The battle marked the conclusion of the Napoleonic Wars and the end of Napoleon's rule, reshaping the European political landscape and heralding the restoration of the Bourbon monarchy in France. The Battle of Waterloo underscores the complexities of military strategy, political alliances, and the enduring legacy of one man's pursuit of power, leaving an indelible imprint on the course of modern European history.

"Napoleon at Waterloo" by Ernest Meissonier is historically intriguing for its portrayal of a pivotal moment during the Battle of Waterloo in 1815. Painted in 1862, the artwork captures Napoleon's somber contemplation amidst the battlefield, reflecting his imminent defeat and the end of his ambitions. Meissonier's attention to detail, color use and atmospheric rendering convey the emotional weight of the event, capturing the complexities of leadership, adversity, and personal reflection in the midst of a decisive battle. The painting offers a poignant glimpse into the inner turmoil of a fallen leader, encapsulating the larger narrative of Napoleon's downfall and the profound impact of the Battle of Waterloo on the trajectory of European history.

On the Evening of the Battle of Waterloo (period: 18 June 1815) by Ernest Crofts, 1877

Painting 40

On the Evening of the
Battle of Waterloo

Ernest Crofts

On the Evening of the Battle of Waterloo holds historical fascination as it encapsulates the aftermath of the decisive conflict that occurred on June 18, 1815. The Battle of Waterloo marked the culmination of the Napoleonic Wars, as Napoleon faced off against a coalition led by the Duke of Wellington and Gebhard Leberecht von Blücher. The battle's outcome led to Napoleon's defeat and subsequent exile to Saint Helena. This event not only signaled the end of Napoleon's dominance but also reshaped the European political landscape. The battle underscored the significance of military strategy, coordination, and the unpredictable nature of warfare. "On the Evening of the Battle of Waterloo" captures the emotional weight of the moment, reflecting the gravity of the conflict's aftermath and the broader historical narrative of ambition, power struggles, and the complex interplay of individuals and events that shaped modern Europe.

"On the Evening of the Battle of Waterloo" by Ernest Crofts is historically captivating for its portrayal of the aftermath of the Battle of Waterloo in 1815. Created in 1877, the painting vividly captures the somber scene as soldiers and civilians reflect on the battlefield's toll. Crofts's attention to detail and emotional resonance conveys the human impact of the conflict, offering a poignant glimpse into the aftermath of warfare. The artwork provides a visual testament to the stark realities faced by individuals on both sides, emphasizing the shared experiences of triumph and tragedy that characterize historical events. Through its evocative portrayal, the painting becomes a reminder of the complexities of war, the resilience of humanity, and the enduring legacy of pivotal moments in history.

Napoleon on Saint Helena (period: 1815 - 1821) by François-Joseph Sandmann, 1820

Painting 41

Napoleon on Saint Helena

François-Joseph Sandmann

Napoleon on Saint Helena is historically compelling as it encapsulates the final chapter of Napoleon Bonaparte's life. Following his defeat at the Battle of Waterloo in 1815, Napoleon was exiled to the remote island of Saint Helena in the South Atlantic by the British government. This marked the culmination of his fall from power and the end of his ambitions. The period of his exile was characterized by isolation, captivity, and intense scrutiny by his British captors. Despite his efforts to maintain his influence and shape his legacy, Napoleon lived out his days in relative seclusion, reflecting on his past achievements and wrestling with his personal frustrations. His presence on Saint Helena underscores the complexities of his rise, rule, and ultimate downfall, as well as the enduring fascination with his larger-than-life persona and the profound impact he left on the course of European history.

"Napoleon on Saint Helena" by François-Joseph Sandmann is historically intriguing for its portrayal of Napoleon's final years in exile. Created in 1820, the artwork captures the subdued atmosphere of Napoleon's time on the remote island after his defeat in 1815. Sandmann's attention to detail and emotive rendering convey the isolation and contemplation that marked this period of exile. The painting becomes a visual reflection on the complexities of Napoleon's legacy, his introspection, and the historical significance of his fall from power. Through the artist's skillful interpretation, the viewer is invited to witness the human dimensions of this once-mighty ruler as he navigated his transition from the pinnacle of power to a life of captivity, shaping the lasting perception of his larger-than-life historical role.

Napoleon on his Deathbed (period: 5 May 1821)
by Horace Vernet, 1826

Painting 42

Napoleon on his Deathbed

Horace Vernet

Napoleon on his deathbed holds profound historical significance as it marks the end of an era and the life of one of the most influential figures in world history. Napoleon's final moments in 1821 on the remote island of Saint Helena symbolize the conclusion of a remarkable journey that saw his rise from Corsican obscurity to becoming Emperor of the French and a global force. His complex legacy encompasses military conquests, significant legal and administrative reforms, and a lasting impact on Europe's political landscape. Napoleon's death also gave rise to debates and discussions about his impact on society, his leadership style, and the enduring allure of his persona. The circumstances of his passing and his subsequent reburial in France reflect the intersection of politics, memory, and the indelible mark he left on history, making his deathbed a poignant and contemplative moment that resonates with historical reflection.

"Napoleon on his Deathbed" by Horace Vernet is historically evocative for its portrayal of the profound and poignant moment of Napoleon's passing in 1821. The artwork captures the solemnity and vulnerability of Napoleon's final hours on the remote island of Saint Helena. Vernet's attention to detail and emotive composition convey the weight of history and the reflective mood surrounding the former emperor's death. The painting serves as a visual meditation on mortality, power, and the complex legacy of a man who had shaped the course of European and global events. Through Vernet's artistic interpretation, viewers are invited to witness the convergence of the personal and the historical, offering a glimpse into the contemplative atmosphere of the time and the enduring impact of Napoleon's life on subsequent generations.

Death of Napoleon (period: 5 May 1821) by Charles de Steuben, 1828

Painting 43

Death of Napoleon

Charles de Steuben

The death of Napoleon Bonaparte in 1821 holds historical significance as it marked the end of an era defined by his ambitious rise and eventual fall from power. Following his exile to the remote island of Saint Helena after his defeat at the Battle of Waterloo, Napoleon spent his final years in relative seclusion and contemplation. His death raised questions of the circumstances surrounding his demise, including rumors of poisoning. His passing symbolized the end of a tumultuous period in European history, characterized by his transformative influence on the continent's political landscape and military conflicts. Napoleon's death also marked the closure of a chapter that had reshaped the world order, leaving a lasting legacy that continues to evoke fascination, debate, and reflection on the complexities of leadership, ambition, and the ebb and flow of historical fortunes.

The depiction of the "Death of Napoleon" by Charles Steuben carries historical resonance as it portrays the final moments of Napoleon's life. The artwork captures the gravity of this significant historical event. Steuben's attention to detail and emotive portrayal encapsulate the somber atmosphere and introspective reflection that marked Napoleon's passing in exile on the remote island of Saint Helena in 1821. The painting becomes a poignant representation of the end of a complex era, reflecting the larger narrative of ambition, power, and the human dimensions of a once-mighty ruler's transition from dominance to mortality. Through Steuben's brushwork, viewers are offered a glimpse into the intersection of history, mortality, and the enduring legacy of a historical figure whose impact continues to reverberate in the collective memory.

Napoleon Reviewing the Guard in the Place du Carrousel (period: 5 May 1821) by Horace Vernet, unknown

Painting 44

Napoleon's Tomb

Horace Vernet

Napoleon's tomb is historically poignant as it serves as the final resting place for one of the most iconic and consequential figures in European history. Located at Les Invalides in Paris, the tomb is a symbol of Napoleon Bonaparte's enduring legacy and impact on the world. After his death in 1821, his body was initially interred on the remote island of Saint Helena. However, in 1840, his remains were returned to France and laid to rest under the grand dome of Les Invalides. The tomb's architectural magnificence, coupled with its historical significance, reinforces Napoleon's status as a monumental figure who left an indelible mark on politics, warfare, and society. The tomb stands as a site of pilgrimage for admirers and historians alike, serving as a tangible reminder of his transformative influence and the complex legacy he left behind.

Napoleon's tomb by Horace Vernet is historically evocative for its portrayal of the final resting place of a monumental figure. Created in the 19th century, the artwork visualizes the tomb at Les Invalides in Paris, where Napoleon Bonaparte was laid to rest. Vernet's attention to detail and atmospheric rendering capture the solemnity and grandeur of the site, echoing the reverence and enduring impact that Napoleon's legacy holds. The painting becomes a visual tribute to the complex legacy of a leader who reshaped Europe's political landscape and military strategies, and it invites viewers to reflect on the historical resonance of his life and the lasting imprint he left on the course of world events.

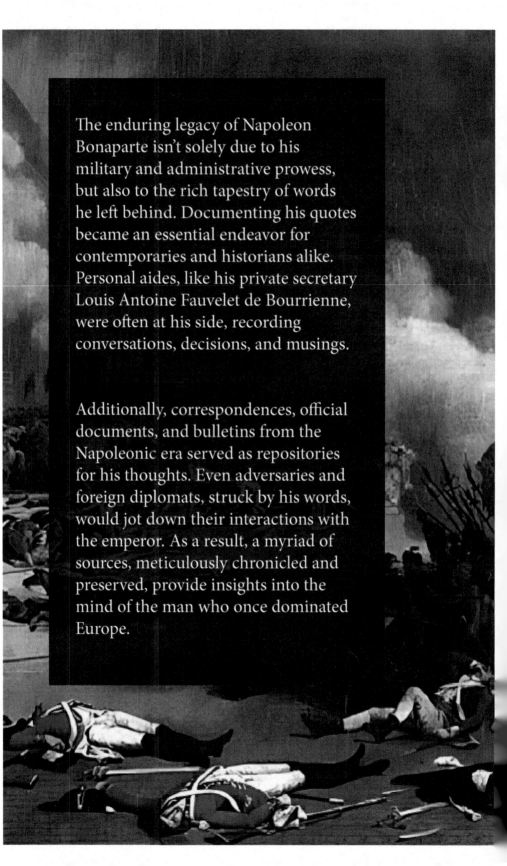

The enduring legacy of Napoleon Bonaparte isn't solely due to his military and administrative prowess, but also to the rich tapestry of words he left behind. Documenting his quotes became an essential endeavor for contemporaries and historians alike. Personal aides, like his private secretary Louis Antoine Fauvelet de Bourrienne, were often at his side, recording conversations, decisions, and musings.

Additionally, correspondences, official documents, and bulletins from the Napoleonic era served as repositories for his thoughts. Even adversaries and foreign diplomats, struck by his words, would jot down their interactions with the emperor. As a result, a myriad of sources, meticulously chronicled and preserved, provide insights into the mind of the man who once dominated Europe.

chapter 2
Quotes

Quote 01

« Victory belongs to the most persevering. »

"Victory belongs to the most persevering" encapsulates his belief that success is not merely a result of talent, strategy, or opportunity, but largely of persistence and tenacity. He posits that victories, whether on the battlefield or in life, are often achieved by those who remain committed and unwavering in their efforts, even in the face of challenges or setbacks. In essence, it's not just about having the right conditions for success, but persistently pursuing one's goals until they are achieved.

Quote 02

« Success is the most convincing talker in the world. »

Through the phrase "Success is the most convincing talker in the world," Napoleon Bonaparte underscores the idea that results speak louder than words. In his perspective, no amount of rhetoric, reasoning, or persuasion can match the influence and credibility of tangible success. When one achieves success, doubts and critiques are often silenced, and the results become the most compelling argument for one's methods, decisions, or strategies. In essence, success validates one's actions and becomes an irrefutable testament to one's capabilities.

Quote 03

« It is only by prudence, wisdom, and dexterity, that great ends are attained and obstacles overcome. Without these qualities nothing succeeds. »

In the statement, "It is only by prudence, wisdom, and dexterity, that great ends are attained and obstacles overcome. Without these qualities nothing succeeds," Napoleon Bonaparte emphasizes the indispensable value of careful planning, acquired knowledge, and skillful execution in achieving significant goals. He suggests that raw ambition or sheer force isn't sufficient; instead, a nuanced combination of foresight (prudence), understanding (wisdom), and adaptability or skill (dexterity) are essential. Without harnessing these three qualities, even the most passionate endeavors are likely to falter.

Quote 04

« Ten people who speak make more noise than
ten thousand who are silent. »

Napoleon's assertion, "Ten people who speak make more
noise than ten thousand who are silent," underscores
the powerful impact of vocal advocacy or dissent over
passive silence. He alludes to the idea that a small group of
individuals, when vocal and determined, can have a more
profound influence on public opinion, societal norms, or
political matters than a much larger group that remains
silent and inactive. Essentially, the quote emphasizes
the significance of active participation and the potential
influence of those who choose to voice their convictions,
regardless of their number.

Quote 05

« Courage isn't having the strength to go on –
it is going on when you don't have strength. »

In his reflection, "Courage isn't having the strength to go on – it is going on when you don't have strength," Napoleon Bonaparte delves into the essence of true bravery. He suggests that courage is not merely a manifestation of physical or mental might, but rather the inner resilience and fortitude to persevere in the face of adversity, exhaustion, or despair. Genuine courage, according to Napoleon, emerges not when one feels strong and invincible, but when one pushes forward despite feeling weak and vulnerable. It's the act of persisting against odds and maintaining one's path even when every fiber of one's being may desire to give up.

Quote 06

« If you want a thing done well,
do it yourself. »

In the statement, "If you want a thing done well, do it yourself," Napoleon Bonaparte highlights the notion of personal responsibility and direct involvement in ensuring the quality of an outcome. He suggests that relying on intermediaries or delegating tasks can sometimes lead to compromises in quality or execution. By taking matters into one's own hands, one can have better control over the precision, dedication, and standards applied to the task. While this sentiment underscores the importance of self-reliance, it also reflects Napoleon's own leadership style, wherein he often took direct command to ensure his vision was realized to his exacting standards.

Quote 07

« I have seen in the most significant of circumstances, that some little thing always decides great events. »

With the statement, "I have seen in the most significant of circumstances, that some little thing always decides great events," Napoleon Bonaparte illuminates the profound influence of seemingly minor details or events on the outcomes of larger, pivotal moments in history. He emphasizes that, even in grand schemes or battles, it is often the overlooked or underestimated factors that can tip the balance. Drawing from his vast military and political experiences, Napoleon recognized that meticulous attention to detail, and the unpredictable nature of events, can have a cascading effect on outcomes, demonstrating that in the grand tapestry of events, even the smallest thread can have a decisive impact.

Quote 08

« It's the unconquerable soul of man, and not the nature of the weapon he uses, that ensures victory. »

In the remark, "It's the unconquerable soul of man, and not the nature of the weapon he uses, that ensures victory," Napoleon Bonaparte is emphasizing the primacy of human spirit, willpower, and determination over mere tools or weaponry in determining the outcome of a conflict. He posits that the intrinsic qualities of a person – their resolve, passion, and spirit – are far more pivotal in achieving success than the external tools at their disposal. To Napoleon, the heart and soul of an individual or an army, their unwavering dedication and commitment, are the true driving forces behind victory, overshadowing even the most advanced or powerful weapons.

Quote 09

« Throw off your worries when you throw off
your clothes at night. »

In the saying, "Throw off your worries when you throw off
your clothes at night," Napoleon Bonaparte conveys the
importance of setting aside one's anxieties and stresses at
the end of the day, emphasizing the rejuvenating power of
rest. Just as one sheds clothing to find physical comfort and
relaxation, one should also mentally unburden themselves
of the day's concerns to find peace of mind. By doing so, an
individual can ensure a restful sleep, recharge effectively,
and approach the subsequent day with renewed energy
and a clear mindset. Essentially, Napoleon underscores the
value of compartmentalizing daily stresses to maintain a
healthy balance between work and rest.

Quote 10

« History is written by the winners. »

In the statement, "History is written by the winners," Napoleon touches upon the idea that those who emerge victorious in conflicts, whether they be military, political, or ideological, often have the power and influence to shape the narrative of events. The victors are able to present their perspectives, justify their actions, and sometimes even diminish or rewrite the contributions and viewpoints of the defeated. Consequently, historical records can be biased, reflecting the perspectives of those in power at the expense of a more objective or comprehensive account. Napoleon's observation serves as a cautionary reminder about the potential subjectivity of historical narratives and the importance of critical engagement with historical sources.

Quote 11

« The truest wisdom is a resolute
determination. »

In the phrase, "The truest wisdom is a resolute
determination," Napoleon Bonaparte accentuates the
importance of unwavering commitment and decisiveness
in achieving one's goals. He suggests that, beyond mere
knowledge or understanding, it's the firmness of purpose
and the determination to see things through that truly
matters. In other words, while intellectual wisdom is
valuable, real wisdom manifests in the capacity to decide
on a course of action and persistently pursue it, even in the
face of challenges. Napoleon believed that a resolute will
could overcome numerous obstacles, and this tenacity was
often the differentiator between success and failure.

Quote 12

« Until you spread your wings, you'll have no
idea how far you can fly. »

With the metaphorical phrase, "Until you spread your
wings, you'll have no idea how far you can fly," Napoleon
Bonaparte emphasizes the concept of untapped potential
and the importance of taking risks. He suggests that one
cannot truly understand their capabilities or the extent
of their potential until they take the initiative, step out of
their comfort zone, and face challenges head-on. By urging
individuals to "spread their wings," Napoleon encourages
taking proactive measures, embarking on new endeavors,
and embracing opportunities, as it is only through such
actions that one can truly gauge their capacity for greatness
and discover the limits of their abilities.

Quote 13

« Variety made the Revolution. Liberty was just a pretext. »

Napoleon Bonaparte's remark, "Variety made the Revolution. Liberty was just a pretext," encapsulates his view that the French Revolution was a result of diverse factors beyond the mere pursuit of liberty. He implied that the revolution's origins were rooted in a complex interplay of economic, social, and political forces, with the ideal of liberty being used as a convenient justification rather than the sole driving force. In essence, he suggested that the revolution's true causes were more intricate and multifaceted than a singular quest for freedom.

Quote 14

« The world suffers a lot. Not because the violence of bad people. But because of the silence of the good people. »

In the statement, "The world suffers a lot. Not because of the violence of bad people. But because of the silence of the good people," Napoleon Bonaparte highlights the profound impact of passivity and inaction by those who know better or possess moral principles. He emphasizes that while malicious acts by a few can indeed cause harm, a greater detriment arises when individuals who have the capacity to stand up for justice, righteousness, or truth choose to remain silent or inactive. Their silence, in effect, enables or tacitly condones the harmful actions of the few. Napoleon's observation serves as a call to action, urging individuals to speak out against injustices and to actively counteract negative forces, rather than passively witnessing them.

Quote 15

« Ability is of little account without
opportunity. »

In the observation, "Ability is of little account without opportunity," Napoleon Bonaparte emphasizes that raw talent or skill, in isolation, isn't enough to achieve greatness or make meaningful contributions. While innate or developed abilities are crucial, they need the right circumstances or platforms to be realized fully and effectively. Without opportunities to apply, test, and refine one's skills, even the most gifted individuals may remain unrecognized or underutilized. Napoleon's statement highlights the symbiotic relationship between individual potential and the external conditions that allow for its expression, underscoring the importance of fostering environments where talent can intersect with opportunity.

Quote 16

« We are made weak both by idleness and
distrust of ourselves. Unfortunate, indeed,
is he who suffers from both. If he is a mere
individual he becomes nothing; if he is a king
he is lost. »

Through the observation, "We are made weak both by
idleness and distrust of ourselves. Unfortunate, indeed,
is he who suffers from both. If he is a mere individual
he becomes nothing; if he is a king he is lost," Napoleon
elucidates the debilitating effects of inaction and self-doubt.
He underscores that the combination of idleness (lack of
purpose or action) and self-distrust (lack of confidence)
can paralyze an individual, rendering them ineffective. For
a common person, this combination leads to obscurity and
unfulfilled potential; for someone in a position of power, like
a king, the consequences are even more dire, as it can lead to
their downfall or ineffectual rule.

Quote 17

« One must change one's tactics every ten years if one wishes to maintain one's superiority. »

In the statement, "One must change one's tactics every ten years if one wishes to maintain one's superiority," Napoleon Bonaparte acknowledges the impermanence of strategies in the face of changing circumstances, technologies, and societal shifts. He highlights that resting on past laurels or rigidly adhering to a once-successful approach can lead to obsolescence and decline. To maintain an edge or superiority, it's vital to adapt, evolve, and reconsider strategies in response to the ever-changing landscape. Napoleon, drawing from his military and leadership experiences, stresses the importance of adaptability and the dangers of complacency for sustained dominance or success.

Quote 18

« The greater the man, the less is he opinionative, he depends upon events and circumstances. »

In the assertion, "The greater the man, the less is he opinionative, he depends upon events and circumstances," Napoleon posits that truly great individuals exhibit a degree of humility and flexibility in their approach, rather than being rigidly anchored to their personal beliefs or opinions. Such individuals recognize that the complexities of life and leadership often require adaptive strategies, molded by unfolding events and prevailing circumstances. In essence, greatness, according to Napoleon, is characterized by a responsive and pragmatic approach, where decisions are informed by the nuances of situations rather than by entrenched viewpoints. This perspective underscores the importance of adaptability and a willingness to shift one's stance when necessary.

Quote 19

« There is one kind of robber whom the law does not strike at, and who steals what is most precious to men: time. »

In the aphorism, "There is one kind of robber whom the law does not strike at, and who steals what is most precious to men: time," Napoleon Bonaparte highlights the inescapable and relentless progression of time, which, unlike tangible possessions, once lost, cannot be reclaimed. He personifies time as a thief, one that operates beyond the jurisdiction of any legal system, subtly drawing attention to its unmatched value. The sentiment underscores the impermanence and finitude of human existence, urging individuals to make the most of their moments, as time, once it slips away, remains the most irrevocable of losses.

Quote 20

« The best cure for the body is a
quiet mind. »

With the statement, "The best cure for the body is a quiet mind," Napoleon Bonaparte emphasizes the deep connection between mental well-being and physical health. He suggests that a tranquil and untroubled mind can have restorative and healing effects on the body. In an era of intense physical demands and stresses, Napoleon recognized that true recuperation and strength stem not just from physical remedies, but significantly from mental peace. This perspective underscores the holistic approach to health, asserting that inner calm and mental clarity can alleviate physical ailments and offer rejuvenation.

Quote 21

« There are but two powers in the world, the sword and the mind. In the long run the sword is always beaten by the mind. »

In his observation, "There are but two powers in the world, the sword and the mind. In the long run, the sword is always beaten by the mind," Napoleon Bonaparte juxtaposes the tangible might of military or violent force (represented by the sword) against the intangible power of intellect, strategy, and ideas (represented by the mind). Napoleon suggests that while immediate victories might be won through brute force, enduring influence and ultimate triumph are achieved through intellectual prowess and ideation. In essence, the raw physicality of the sword, no matter how dominant, is eventually surpassed by the enduring and pervasive influence of the mind's capabilities, be it in strategy, innovation, or persuasion.

Quote 22

« Men take only their needs into consideration
– never their abilities. »

In the statement, "Men take only their needs into consideration – never their abilities," Napoleon Bonaparte underscores the notion that individuals often focus on their immediate desires and necessities without fully contemplating or leveraging their inherent talents and potential. He implies that people might limit their ambitions or aspirations based on perceived needs or immediate challenges, rather than pushing themselves to explore and harness the full extent of their abilities. Napoleon's sentiment serves as a commentary on human nature and a reminder that one should not solely act based on immediate necessities, but should also recognize and utilize their intrinsic capabilities to achieve greater feats.

Quote 23

« Nothing is more difficult, and therefore more precious, than to be able to decide. »

In the maxim, "Nothing is more difficult, and therefore more precious, than to be able to decide," Napoleon Bonaparte emphasizes the inherent challenge and value in making decisive choices. Decision-making often requires weighing multiple factors, confronting uncertainties, and sometimes even facing unpalatable trade-offs. Yet, the ability to arrive at a clear decision, especially under pressure or in complex situations, is an invaluable skill. Napoleon, drawing from his own leadership experiences, recognizes that decisiveness not only shapes outcomes but also demonstrates a leader's mettle and character. In essence, the capacity to decide, despite its challenges, is a hallmark of leadership and a critical factor in achieving success and commanding respect.

Quote 24

« Take time to deliberate, but when the time for
action comes, stop thinking and go in. »

In the directive, "Take time to deliberate, but when
the time for action comes, stop thinking and go in,"
Napoleon Bonaparte encapsulates a philosophy of
balanced leadership. He stresses the importance of careful
consideration, reflection, and planning when faced with
significant choices. However, he equally emphasizes
that once decisions are made, it's crucial to act with
determination and resolve, setting aside over-analysis or
second-guessing. Napoleon's wisdom underscores that
while thoughtful deliberation is key to informed decision-
making, effective leadership also requires the courage to
act decisively and commit to one's chosen course, even in
the face of uncertainties.

Quote 25

« The reason most people fail instead of succeed is they trade what they want most for what they want at the moment. »

In his observation, "The reason most people fail instead of succeed is they trade what they want most for what they want at the moment," Napoleon Bonaparte highlights the common human tendency towards immediate gratification at the expense of long-term goals. He suggests that individuals often make choices that offer fleeting satisfaction or momentary relief, neglecting their overarching aspirations or enduring objectives. This inclination to prioritize the immediate over the eventual can derail one's path to genuine success. Napoleon's insight underscores the importance of discipline, foresight, and staying committed to one's primary goals, even when faced with tempting diversions or short-term rewards.

Quote 26

« Death is nothing, but to live defeated and inglorious is to die daily. »

In the profound statement, "Death is nothing, but to live defeated and inglorious is to die daily," Napoleon Bonaparte conveys the sentiment that physical death is not the ultimate tragedy in life. Instead, a life lived in perpetual defeat, without honor or purpose, is a more grievous fate, akin to experiencing the pain of death every single day. For Napoleon, who prized glory, ambition, and achievement, the idea of living without these attributes was tantamount to a prolonged demise of the spirit and ambition. His words serve as a compelling reminder of the importance of living with purpose, passion, and honor, emphasizing that a life without these elements might be a fate worse than death itself.

Quote 27

« As a rule it is circumstances that make men. »

In the statement, "As a rule it is circumstances that make men," Napoleon Bonaparte underscores the influential role that external situations, events, and environments play in shaping an individual's character, decisions, and destiny. He suggests that while inherent traits and talents matter, it is often the crucible of circumstances that truly tests, refines, and defines a person. For Napoleon, who rose from relatively humble origins to become Emperor of the French, circumstances—ranging from political upheavals to military challenges—played a pivotal role in his ascension and the formation of his legacy. His observation serves as a testament to the transformative power of external forces in an individual's life, emphasizing that greatness is often forged in the fires of adversity and opportunity.

Quote 28

« Courage cannot be counterfeited. It is one
virtue that escapes hypocrisy. »

In the statement, "Courage cannot be counterfeited. It is
one virtue that escapes hypocrisy," Napoleon Bonaparte
highlights the unique authenticity of courage as a virtue.
He emphasizes that while many qualities can be feigned
or superficially presented, true courage stands distinct,
manifesting itself unmistakably in action, especially in
challenging times. Courage, according to Napoleon, is
genuine and cannot be merely mimicked for show; it's
a deeply-rooted quality that reveals itself in the face of
adversity. By asserting this, he underscores the idea that
genuine bravery is both rare and unmistakable, and that
it remains immune to the pretenses that might taint other
virtues.

Quote 29

« Space I can recover. Time, never. »

In the reflection, "Space I can recover. Time, never," Napoleon Bonaparte captures the irreversible nature of time in contrast to the reclaimable nature of territorial or spatial losses. Drawing from his military and leadership experiences, Napoleon recognized that while lost ground in battle could be regained with strategy and effort, time, once passed, is gone forever and cannot be retrieved or replayed. His statement emphasizes the inherent value and finiteness of time, urging an appreciation for its passage and a focus on making judicious use of every moment, especially in the realm of decision-making and action.

Quote 30

« The battlefield is a scene of constant chaos. The winner will be the one who controls that chaos, both his own and the enemies. »

In the declaration, "The battlefield is a scene of constant chaos. The winner will be the one who controls that chaos, both his own and the enemies," Napoleon Bonaparte articulates the inherent unpredictability and turmoil present in warfare. He emphasizes that victory does not merely go to the strongest or most equipped, but to those who can best manage and harness the disorder—navigating their internal challenges, fears, and uncertainties, while simultaneously exploiting or countering the chaos confronting them from the enemy. Napoleon's insight, rooted in his vast military experience, speaks to the broader principle that success often hinges on one's ability to manage complexity and unpredictability, turning chaotic scenarios into strategic advantages.

Quote 31

« I make my battle plans from the spirit of my sleeping soldiers. »

In the statement, "I make my battle plans from the spirit of my sleeping soldiers," Napoleon Bonaparte conveys the profound importance he placed on the morale, well-being, and determination of his troops. Rather than basing his strategies solely on abstract tactical considerations, he took into account the emotional and physical state of his soldiers. The "spirit" of the sleeping soldiers symbolizes their resilience, determination, and trust in their leader. Napoleon recognized that the strength and spirit of his army were pivotal to any battle's outcome. This sentiment underscores the idea that true leadership entails a deep connection to and understanding of one's team, recognizing that their collective spirit and morale can be as decisive as any tactical maneuver.

Quote 32

« You don't reason with intellectuals.
You shoot them. »

The statement, "You don't reason with intellectuals. You shoot them," attributed to Napoleon Bonaparte, speaks to his skepticism towards intellectuals, whom he might have viewed as potential sources of dissent or challenges to his authority. This provocative sentiment underscores the tension between autocratic rule and intellectual critique. Intellectuals, by their nature, question, analyze, and often challenge prevailing norms and authorities. For a ruler who aimed for centralized control and unity, such dissenting voices could be perceived as threats. In a broader context, the quote encapsulates the age-old tension between power and free thought, suggesting that rulers might sometimes prefer silencing critique rather than engaging with it.

Quote 33

« Soldiers generally win battles; generals get credit for them. »

In the observation, "Soldiers generally win battles; generals get credit for them," Napoleon Bonaparte draws attention to the often-overlooked contributions of the rank-and-file soldiers in the outcome of battles and the disproportionate recognition that leadership, specifically generals, receive. While generals strategize and command, it's the soldiers on the ground who face the immediate dangers and make the direct actions needed for victory. Napoleon, himself a general and later an emperor, acknowledges this disparity in recognition, highlighting the valor and efforts of the common soldier. The statement underscores the broader theme of many hierarchical systems, where those at the top often receive accolades for the collective efforts and sacrifices of those they lead.

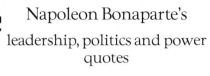

Quote 34

« A throne is only a bench covered
with velvet. »

In the aphorism, "A throne is only a bench covered with velvet," Napoleon Bonaparte offers a stripped-down view of the symbols of power and authority. By reducing a throne—a symbol of majesty, dominion, and sovereignty—to a mere "bench," albeit adorned, Napoleon underscores the idea that power and leadership roles are, at their core, positions of responsibility rather than just privilege. The velvet represents the external trappings and luxuries of power, which can be deceptive in masking the true nature and challenges of leadership. The statement serves as a reminder that, beyond the glamour and prestige, leadership often demands sacrifice, resilience, and decision-making, and that one should not be blinded by its outward manifestations.

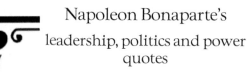

Quote 35

« The army is the true nobility of our country. »

In proclaiming, "The army is the true nobility of our country," Napoleon Bonaparte emphasizes the paramount importance and honor he places on the military, elevating its status above even the traditional aristocracy. Napoleon, who rose to prominence through military ranks and whose empire was built on the strength of his armies, believed in the virtue, loyalty, and significance of the military institution. By contrasting the army with the "nobility," traditionally seen as the elite class, he underscores the idea that true nobility is not just about birthright or inherited status but is earned through service, sacrifice, and dedication to the nation. His statement encapsulates the deep respect he had for the soldiers and their role in shaping and defending the nation's destiny.

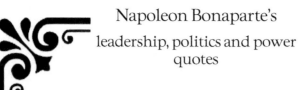

Quote 36

« France has more need of me than I have need
of France. »

In the declaration, "France has more need of me than I
have need of France," Napoleon Bonaparte expresses his
profound belief in his indispensability to the French nation.
The statement carries an undertone of self-assuredness and
even arrogance, emphasizing Napoleon's conviction that
his leadership, vision, and governance were essential to
France's prosperity, stability, and global stature. By placing
the nation's needs below his own, he conveys the sentiment
that while he could survive or even thrive without France,
the country would struggle without his guidance. This
perspective reflects Napoleon's immense self-confidence
and his view of his pivotal role in the historical and political
trajectory of France.

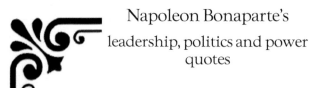

Quote 37

« In politics, stupidity is not a handicap. »

With the statement, "In politics, stupidity is not a handicap," Napoleon Bonaparte offers a wry observation on the political landscape, suggesting that political success does not always correlate with intelligence or wisdom. He implies that other factors, such as charisma, populism, or manipulation, can compensate for a lack of understanding or clear-sightedness in political arenas. Furthermore, the statement could also hint at the public's occasional propensity to support or be swayed by leaders or policies that may not necessarily be in their best interests. In essence, Napoleon points out the paradoxes and unpredictabilities inherent in politics, where reason and foresight aren't always the driving forces behind success or influence.

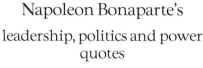

Quote 38

« I saw the crown of France laying on the
ground, so I picked it up with my sword. »

In the declaration, "I saw the crown of France laying on
the ground, so I picked it up with my sword," Napoleon
Bonaparte vividly encapsulates his rapid rise to power
amidst the political turmoil that engulfed France post-
Revolution. This metaphor underscores his seizing of
opportunity: the "crown" symbolizes leadership and
authority, while the "sword" represents military prowess.
Napoleon, having risen through the military ranks,
effectively utilized his martial achievements to cement
his political dominance. The statement paints a picture of
France's power vacuum and instability, and how Napoleon,
through strategic might and determination, positioned
himself as the nation's savior and leader. It underscores his
belief in destiny, ambition, and the role of force in
shaping history.

Quote 39

« Power is my mistress. I have worked too hard
at her conquest to allow anyone to take her
away from me. »

Napoleon Bonaparte's assertion, "Power is my mistress.
I have worked too hard at her conquest to allow anyone
to take her away from me," vividly conveys his intense
and personal relationship with power. By personifying
power as a "mistress," he likens his pursuit of authority to
a romantic or passionate endeavor, suggesting both his
deep attachment to it and the sacrifices he made for it. The
emphasis on his hard work and "conquest" denotes the
challenges he faced, his strategic acumen, and the relentless
ambition that propelled his ascent. The declaration
underscores his protective, even possessive, stance
toward his achieved dominance, revealing a ruler fiercely
determined not to lose what he fought so ardently to obtain.

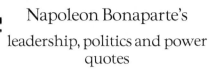

Quote 40

« In politics… never retreat, never retract…
never admit a mistake. »

In the statement, "In politics… never retreat, never retract…
never admit a mistake," Napoleon Bonaparte provides
insight into his approach to political strategy and leadership.
He emphasizes the importance of maintaining a facade of
unwavering confidence and infallibility in the treacherous
realm of politics. By advising against retreating or retracting,
he suggests that showing perceived weakness or indecision
can be exploited by opponents. Similarly, by recommending
against admitting mistakes, he alludes to the notion that
acknowledging errors can diminish a leader's authority and
credibility in the eyes of the public or political adversaries.
Essentially, Napoleon underscores the importance of
perception in politics, implying that a leader's strength
often lies as much in their projected image as in
their actual decisions or actions.

Quote 41

« The great difficulty with politics is, that there
are no established principles. »

In the observation, "The great difficulty with politics is, that
there are no established principles," Napoleon Bonaparte
addresses the fluid and often unpredictable nature of the
political landscape. He points out the absence of steadfast
rules or enduring truths in politics, implying that politicians
often need to adapt, maneuver, and even compromise
based on changing circumstances, public opinion, and
shifting alliances. Unlike scientific fields where principles
remain consistent, politics, according to Napoleon, is an
arena where strategies and stances may need to be altered
based on the prevailing situation. This inherent instability
challenges leaders to be agile and pragmatic, rather than
rigidly adhering to a single doctrine or ideology.

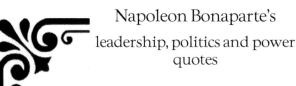

Quote 42

« I love power like a musician loves music. »

With the analogy, "I love power like a musician loves music," Napoleon Bonaparte poetically communicates his profound affinity for power. Just as a musician is deeply connected to music, finding expression, purpose, and fulfillment in it, Napoleon felt a similar passion and intrinsic connection to the realms of authority and control. The comparison underscores that for him, the pursuit and exercise of power was not merely a means to an end, but an endeavor he relished, much like an artist revels in their craft. In this light, power for Napoleon was both an art and a vocation, a source of inspiration and purpose, and not just a vehicle for ambition.

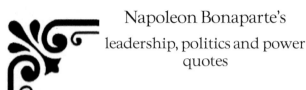

Quote 43

« I can no longer obey; I have tasted command,
and I cannot give it up. »

In the statement, "I can no longer obey; I have tasted command, and I cannot give it up," Napoleon Bonaparte reveals the transformative nature of leadership and the profound impact it had on him. Having risen to the pinnacle of power and having experienced the allure and authority of command, he confesses an inability to revert to a subservient role. Napoleon's words capture the intoxication of leadership, the seductive pull of being in control, and making pivotal decisions. The statement underscores the idea that once someone has tasted the unparalleled influence and autonomy of leadership, it becomes exceedingly challenging to relinquish it or to accept a lesser position, reflecting the profound transformation that power can evoke in an individual's disposition and aspirations.

Quote 44

« A Constitution should be short and obscure. »

In saying, "A Constitution should be short and obscure," Napoleon Bonaparte articulates a shrewd, perhaps cynical, perspective on governance and control. By advocating for a brief and ambiguous constitution, he hints at the utility of keeping the foundational law open to interpretation, which would allow those in power greater flexibility and discretion in its application. A vague constitution can be molded and adjusted to fit the evolving needs or desires of a ruling authority, thereby avoiding potential constraints or challenges to its decisions. Napoleon's sentiment speaks to a strategic approach where the clarity that citizens might seek in a constitution is sacrificed for the latitude it offers leaders, allowing them to navigate and shape governance without stringent checks and balances.

Quote 45

« I am sometimes a fox and sometimes a lion. The whole secret of government lies in knowing when to be the one or the other. »

In the statement, "I am sometimes a fox and sometimes a lion. The whole secret of government lies in knowing when to be the one or the other," Napoleon Bonaparte underscores the duality and adaptability required in leadership. The fox symbolizes cunning, strategy, and intelligence, while the lion represents strength, authority, and direct confrontation. Napoleon suggests that effective governance isn't about consistently employing one approach, but about astutely discerning which tactic is needed in a given situation. Leaders must be adept at both subtle maneuvering and decisive action, and the art of statesmanship lies in understanding when to employ guile and when to wield power outright. It's a testament to the complex balance of diplomacy and force in leadership.

Quote 46

« You become strong by defying defeat and by
turning loss and failure into success. »

Through the statement, "You become strong by defying
defeat and by turning loss and failure into success,"
Napoleon Bonaparte highlights the transformative power
of adversity and the resilience of the human spirit. He
asserts that true strength isn't born from consistent victory
but from confronting and overcoming challenges. Facing
defeat and setbacks, instead of succumbing to them, can
forge a resilience and determination that ultimately drives
success. It's the process of learning from failures, adapting,
and emerging even more resolute that defines greatness.
In essence, Napoleon champions the idea that it's not the
absence of failure that makes one strong, but the ability to
turn those very failures into stepping stones towards
triumph.

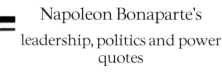

Quote 47

« Public opinion is the thermometer a monarch should constantly consult. »

In the assertion, "Public opinion is the thermometer a monarch should constantly consult," Napoleon acknowledges the pivotal role that public sentiment plays in governance, even in autocratic regimes. Comparing public opinion to a thermometer, he suggests that it serves as an essential gauge that measures the mood and sentiments of the populace. By regularly consulting this "thermometer," a monarch can ascertain the acceptability of his policies, anticipate potential unrest or resistance, and adapt strategies to ensure stability and continuity of his reign. While Napoleon often wielded power with an iron fist, this statement reveals his astute recognition of the need to remain attuned to the pulse of the people, understanding that their perception and sentiment could influence the success or downfall of even the mightiest of rulers.

Quote 48

« Always carry champagne! In victory You
deserve it & in defeat You need it! »

Through the whimsical advice, "Always carry champagne!
In victory you deserve it & in defeat you need it!", Napoleon
Bonaparte extols the dual utility of celebrating highs and
comforting oneself during lows. He underlines the human
need to commemorate achievements and revel in the joy of
success — moments when one "deserves" the effervescence
of champagne. Conversely, in the face of setbacks or
defeats, the same bubbly drink serves as a solace, a means
to uplift spirits and find resilience amidst disappointments.
Napoleon's quote, while light-hearted, underscores a deeper
philosophy: life is a mixture of triumphs and tribulations,
and one must always find reasons to cherish moments or
seek comfort, ensuring that the spirit remains undeterred
regardless of circumstances.

Quote 49

« Those who receive the most images into their memories have the most lively imaginations. »

In the statement, "Those who receive the most images into their memories have the most lively imaginations," Napoleon Bonaparte touches upon the intrinsic link between memory and creativity. He proposes that individuals who absorb and retain a plethora of experiences, sights, and learnings possess a richer reservoir of 'images' or ideas from which to draw upon. This abundant mental tapestry, in turn, fuels a vibrant imagination, allowing such individuals to think divergently, connect disparate ideas, and innovate. Essentially, Napoleon celebrates the idea that a well-stocked mind, filled with diverse memories and experiences, becomes a fertile ground for creative thought and groundbreaking ideas.

Quote 50

« Never interrupt your enemy when he is
making a mistake. »

In the adage, "Never interrupt your enemy when he is
making a mistake," Napoleon Bonaparte encapsulates a
fundamental principle of strategic wisdom. He suggests that
when adversaries are on a path of self-destruction or are
committing errors, it is in one's best interest to stand back
and allow those mistakes to play out rather than intervening
and potentially altering their course. Intervening might
provide the enemy with an opportunity to correct their
course, regroup, or devise a new strategy. By allowing them
to continue their missteps unhindered, one maximizes their
own advantage and strengthens their position. Napoleon's
words emphasize patience, discernment, and the value of
using an opponent's weaknesses to one's own benefit in
warfare, politics, and beyond.

Quote 51

« Skepticism is a virtue in history as well as in philosophy. »

Through the statement, "Skepticism is a virtue in history as well as in philosophy," Napoleon Bonaparte underscores the importance of critical thinking and questioning established narratives. In philosophy, skepticism serves as a tool to challenge assumptions and probe the validity of claims, ensuring that beliefs are well-founded. Similarly, in the realm of history, where events are often colored by the perspectives of those recording them, skepticism prompts historians to critically assess sources, consider biases, and seek multiple viewpoints to approach a more holistic and accurate understanding. Napoleon's assertion reminds us that accepting information at face value, without scrutiny, can lead to misconceptions; a discerning, skeptical approach ensures that knowledge is both rigorous and robust.

Quote 52

« The greatest danger occurs at the moment of victory. »

In the assertion "The greatest danger occurs at the moment of victory," Napoleon Bonaparte highlights a nuanced understanding of triumphs. While victory is typically associated with celebration and relief, Napoleon warns of the vulnerabilities it can expose. Winning can sometimes lead to complacency, overconfidence, or a lack of preparedness for subsequent challenges. A victorious party might drop their guard, thinking the hardest part is behind them, only to be taken by surprise by new threats or overlooked repercussions. Napoleon's wisdom suggests that in the very moment of triumph, one should remain vigilant, cautious, and forward-looking, understanding that success can sometimes sow the seeds of future downfalls if not managed with prudence.

Quote 53

« I start out by believing the worst. »

In declaring "I start out by believing the worst," Napoleon
Bonaparte sheds light on his strategic approach to
situations, emphasizing caution and preparedness.
By assuming the worst-case scenario from the outset,
Napoleon would be primed to preempt challenges, foresee
potential pitfalls, and develop strategies to counteract
them. This perspective is rooted in pragmatism; by
preparing for the most adverse circumstances, one ensures
that they're equipped to handle less severe challenges with
relative ease. Napoleon's statement underscores the value of
cautious optimism in leadership, where the best outcomes
arise from preparing for the worst while striving for the
best.

Quote 54

« Never depend on the multitude, full of instability and whims; always take precautions against it. »

In the statement, "Never depend on the multitude, full of instability and whims; always take precautions against it," Napoleon Bonaparte underscores the unpredictability and fickle nature of crowds or popular opinion. He warns against placing too much trust or reliance on the collective sentiments of the masses, as they can be swayed by emotions, momentary impulses, or fleeting trends. Instead of depending solely on the favor of the majority, leaders and decision-makers should be wary and prepared for shifts in popular sentiment. Napoleon's cautionary advice emphasizes the need for leaders to remain steadfast in their convictions and to have contingency plans, understanding that the tide of public opinion can turn quickly and unexpectedly.

Quote 55

« The best way to keep one's word
is not to give it. »

With the phrase "The best way to keep one's word is not to give it," Napoleon Bonaparte conveys a profound lesson in prudence and restraint. He suggests that commitments and promises carry weight and should not be made lightly. By refraining from hastily pledging one's word, an individual ensures they never fall short of their promises or overcommit themselves. This perspective underscores the importance of considering the implications and responsibilities that come with making commitments. Essentially, Napoleon advises that it's better to be cautious in offering guarantees than to risk breaking them, as a reputation for reliability and trustworthiness is invaluable.

Quote 56

« When you have an enemy in your power,
deprive him of the means of ever
injuring you. »

In the dictum "When you have an enemy in your power,
deprive him of the means of ever injuring you," Napoleon
Bonaparte articulates a strategy of ensuring long-term
security by neutralizing the potential threats posed by
defeated adversaries. He emphasizes the prudence of not
leaving room for future reprisals, suggesting that it's wise to
curtail an enemy's capacity to cause harm even after their
immediate defeat. This approach aligns with the principles
of strategic thinking, recognizing that vulnerabilities, if
left unchecked, could lead to resurgence or retaliation.
Napoleon's counsel underscores the importance of
thoroughness in dealing with adversaries, a concept often
applied in military and political contexts to prevent the
resurgence of threats.

Quote 57

« You must not fight too often with one enemy, or you will teach him all your art of war. »

In the adage "You must not fight too often with one enemy, or you will teach him all your art of war," Napoleon Bonaparte underscores the need for strategic restraint and diversity in military engagements. He advises against repetitive conflicts with the same adversary, as the familiarity bred by frequent encounters can lead them to anticipate and counter one's tactics effectively. By sparingly engaging, a leader preserves an element of surprise and maintains the upper hand in their approach. Napoleon's wisdom reflects the notion that unpredictability and adaptability are essential components of successful warfare, highlighting the importance of keeping opponents off balance and preventing them from fully deciphering one's strategies.

Napoleon Bonaparte's
strategy quotes

Quote 58

« There are only two forces that unite men –
fear and interest. »

With the declaration "There are only two forces that unite
men – fear and interest," Napoleon Bonaparte succinctly
captures the fundamental motivators of human behavior.
He simplifies the complex web of influences by highlighting
that individuals tend to be driven by either self-preservation
stemming from fear or personal gain arising from self-
interest. This observation resonates with the realms of
politics, power dynamics, and social interactions. Napoleon's
assertion reflects an understanding of the powerful
psychological and economic forces that underpin human
actions, asserting that fear of consequences and the pursuit
of personal benefit often guide individuals and shape the
dynamics of societies and nations.

Quote 59

« There are only two forces that unite men –
fear and interest. »

In the assertion "There are only two forces that unite
men – fear and interest," Napoleon Bonaparte distills
human motivations to their core elements. He suggests
that individuals are primarily driven by self-preservation,
represented by fear, and self-advancement, represented by
interest. Napoleon's observation delves into the fundamental
aspects of human nature that influence behavior and
decisions. By highlighting these two driving forces, he offers
a simple yet insightful framework for understanding why
people act the way they do in various contexts, be it personal
relationships, politics, economics, or societal interactions.
The statement encapsulates a pragmatic view of human
psychology and forms a basis for comprehending the
dynamics of human behavior and interactions
on a broader scale.

Quote 60

« Religion is excellent stuff for keeping common people quiet. Religion is what keeps the poor from murdering the rich. »

With the statement, "Religion is excellent stuff for keeping common people quiet. Religion is what keeps the poor from murdering the rich," Napoleon Bonaparte expressed a utilitarian and cynical view of religion as a mechanism of social control. He suggested that religion serves to pacify the masses and maintain the existing power structures. By emphasizing virtues like obedience, humility, and acceptance of one's fate, religious teachings, in Napoleon's perspective, deter societal unrest and potential uprisings against the elite. Essentially, he viewed religion not primarily as a spiritual or moral force but as a tool that ensures the stability and longevity of the established order by mitigating class tensions.

Quote 61

« Let France have good mothers, and she will
have good sons. »

With the declaration "Let France have good mothers, and
she will have good sons," Napoleon Bonaparte underscores
the influential role of mothers in shaping the character and
values of future generations. By focusing on the nurturing
and upbringing provided by mothers, he emphasizes
their impact on the development of virtuous and capable
individuals. Napoleon's sentiment suggests that the qualities
instilled in children during their formative years, especially
by their mothers, contribute significantly to their moral
compass, resilience, and potential for greatness. This maxim
underscores the importance of maternal guidance in
nurturing a strong and principled citizenry, highlighting the
pivotal role that women play in the stability and prosperity
of a nation.

Quote 62

« The future destiny of a child is always the
work of the mother. »

In the statement "The future destiny of a child is always
the work of the mother," Napoleon Bonaparte emphasizes
the profound influence mothers have on shaping the lives
and potential of their children. He underscores the idea
that a child's upbringing, values, and early experiences
largely stem from their maternal care and guidance.
Napoleon's sentiment underscores the pivotal role of
mothers as educators, nurturers, and role models who
lay the foundation for a child's character, aspirations, and
accomplishments. This perspective underscores the far-
reaching impact of maternal influence and the enduring
legacy it can leave on the generations that follow.

Quote 63

« One should never forbid what one lacks the
power to prevent. »

In the assertion "One should never forbid what one
lacks the power to prevent," Napoleon Bonaparte offers
a pragmatic insight into leadership and authority. He
suggests that imposing prohibitions without the ability
to enforce them is counterproductive, as it undermines
one's credibility and control. By acknowledging the
limitations of one's power, Napoleon advises leaders to
choose their battles wisely and only exert authority where
they can ensure compliance. This advice highlights the
importance of strategic decision-making and the need for
leaders to project authority within the boundaries of their
capabilities, avoiding situations that could weaken their
influence or provoke defiance.

Quote 64

« The surest way to remain poor is to be an
honest man. »

In the declaration "The surest way to remain poor is to be
an honest man," Napoleon Bonaparte presents a somewhat
cynical perspective on the challenges of socio-economic
advancement. He suggests that adhering strictly to principles
of honesty and integrity can sometimes hinder financial
prosperity, particularly in environments where less scrupulous
individuals may exploit loopholes or cut corners for personal
gain. Napoleon's statement underscores the complexities
of navigating ethical considerations in pursuit of success,
implying that the pursuit of integrity might entail sacrifices,
especially in situations where dishonest practices seem to
offer expedient advantages. This assertion encapsulates a
sobering commentary on the intersections of
ethics, opportunity, and material success.

Quote 65

« The great proof of madness is the disproportion of one's designs to one's means. »

In the assertion "The great proof of madness is the disproportion of one's designs to one's means," Napoleon Bonaparte articulates a criterion to identify impractical or irrational ambitions. He suggests that when a person's aspirations or plans far exceed their available resources, capabilities, or realistic avenues for achievement, it serves as a telltale sign of folly. Napoleon's observation underscores the importance of aligning ambitions with practical means and recognizing the limitations of one's resources. This maxim reflects a practical approach to goal-setting, urging individuals to pursue objectives that are within the realm of attainability, thus avoiding unnecessary risks and disappointment caused by overreaching.

Quote 66

« True character stands the test of emergencies.
Do not be mistaken, it is weakness from which
the awakening is rude. »

In the adage "True character stands the test of emergencies.
Do not be mistaken, it is weakness from which the
awakening is rude," Napoleon Bonaparte underscores the
notion that one's authentic character becomes evident
in times of crisis or adversity. He implies that facing
challenges reveals whether a person possesses strength,
resilience, and integrity or if they succumb to weakness.
Napoleon's insight underscores the importance of fortitude
and authenticity, cautioning against misjudging one's true
nature during periods of relative calm. By highlighting the
potential harsh reality of discovering one's vulnerabilities,
he emphasizes the importance of cultivating inner strength
and moral fiber to navigate through difficult situations with
grace and composure.

Quote 67

« The French complain of everything, and
always. »

In the observation "The French complain of everything, and always," Napoleon Bonaparte captures a cultural tendency for continuous discontent and criticism. He highlights a perceived inclination among the French populace to express dissatisfaction about various aspects of life persistently and without relent. This statement can be interpreted as a commentary on the perceived national temperament or a reflection on the intricacies of social dynamics. Napoleon's words touch on the complexity of public sentiment, suggesting that dissatisfaction might be deeply ingrained in the cultural fabric, possibly arising from historical, political, or societal factors.

Napoleon Bonaparte's
general quotes

Quote 68

« Show me a family of readers, and I will show
you the people who move the world. »

With the statement "Show me a family of readers, and I
will show you the people who move the world," Napoleon
Bonaparte underscores the transformative power of
education and knowledge. He suggests that individuals
who cultivate a habit of reading and intellectual exploration
possess the tools to shape and influence the course of
history. By highlighting the link between an engaged,
informed populace and societal progress, Napoleon implies
that readers are equipped to think critically, envision
change, and engage in conversations that drive innovation
and advancement. This maxim underscores the enduring
importance of fostering a culture of learning and curiosity
within families and communities, recognizing the potential
for educated individuals to be catalysts for positive
change on a broader scale.

Quote 69

« A woman laughing is a woman
conquered. »

In the assertion "A woman laughing is a woman conquered," Napoleon Bonaparte reflects a view on the dynamics of charm and conquest. He suggests that a woman's laughter, often interpreted as a sign of happiness and receptiveness, can be perceived as a form of conquest by those seeking to win her affection or attention. This phrase alludes to the idea that a woman's amusement or responsiveness can signify a certain level of vulnerability or openness, which some might exploit for their own purposes. It's important to note that this phrase carries a historical context and perspective that might not align with contemporary views on relationships and interactions.

Quote 70

« The poor man and the beggar are two quite different classes: one commands respect, the other arouses anger. »

In the statement "The poor man and the beggar are two quite different classes: one commands respect, the other arouses anger," Napoleon Bonaparte draws a distinction between individuals who face financial hardship. He suggests that while being poor does not necessarily diminish one's dignity or self-worth, begging can evoke negative sentiments due to the perception of dependence or the act of seeking charity. Napoleon's observation reflects a societal attitude of his time, highlighting the nuanced perceptions that can arise from economic disparity. He implies that the act of begging might be viewed as intrusive or degrading, potentially engendering resentment, while someone facing poverty without resorting to begging retains a sense of agency and self-respect that can inspire empathy or admiration.

Quote 71

« Friends must always be treated as if one day
they might be enemies. »

Napoleon Bonaparte's assertion, "Friends must always be
treated as if one day they might be enemies," speaks to his
keen sense of the unpredictable nature of political alliances
and human relationships. Drawing from his vast experience
in the tumultuous arenas of military campaigns and political
maneuverings, Napoleon emphasizes the importance of
caution and foresight. Even close allies can, under changing
circumstances, become adversaries. By advising such a
guarded approach, Napoleon underscores the transient
nature of power and loyalty, suggesting that one should
always be prepared for shifts in allegiance and the inherent
unpredictability of both personal and political relationships.
This perspective reflects the volatile and often treacherous
landscape of power dynamics in which he operated.

Quote 72

« It is the cause, not the death, that makes the martyr. »

In the statement "It is the cause, not the death, that makes the martyr," Napoleon Bonaparte emphasizes the importance of purpose and conviction in determining the significance of sacrifice. He suggests that it's not the act of dying itself, but the underlying cause or belief for which one is willing to lay down their life, that confers the status of martyrdom. Napoleon's sentiment underscores the idea that the value of an individual's sacrifice is tied to the principles they uphold, highlighting the power of dedication and the enduring impact of a noble cause. This perspective resonates with the broader notion that the depth of commitment to an idea or ideal is what defines the lasting legacy of those who give their lives for it.

Quote 73

« The hand that gives is among the hand that takes. Money has no fatherland, financiers are without patriotism and without decency, their sole object is gain. »

In the statement "The hand that gives is among the hand that takes. Money has no fatherland, financiers are without patriotism and without decency, their sole object is gain," Napoleon Bonaparte addresses the complex nature of finance and the potential motives behind financial dealings. He suggests that those involved in financial transactions often operate in a realm where personal gain transcends national allegiance or ethical considerations. Napoleon's words hint at the idea that financial interests can sometimes supersede loyalty to one's country, and he implies that financiers may prioritize profits over principles. This view underscores a skepticism about the motivations of those immersed in financial pursuits, questioning the extent to which monetary interests can shape behaviors and priorities independent of broader societal concerns.

Quote 74

« Courage is like love, it must have hope for nourishment. »

In the analogy "Courage is like love, it must have hope for nourishment," Napoleon Bonaparte draws a parallel between two powerful emotions or attributes. He suggests that, similar to how love draws sustenance from hope and positivity, courage also thrives when fueled by optimism and the anticipation of favorable outcomes. Napoleon's comparison underscores the psychological interplay between emotions and motivations, implying that maintaining hope can invigorate one's resolve to confront challenges and persevere in the face of adversity. This insight underscores the interconnectedness of emotions and their impact on personal strength and determination.

Quote 75

« Four hostile newspapers are more to be feared than a thousand bayonets. »

In the statement "Four hostile newspapers are more to be feared than a thousand bayonets," Napoleon Bonaparte underscores the potent influence of media and public opinion in shaping perceptions and driving change.
He suggests that a handful of critical or oppositional newspapers can wield more power than a substantial military force. This viewpoint reflects the recognition of the sway that information and public discourse hold in society. Napoleon's insight anticipates the pivotal role of media in shaping public sentiment, raising awareness, and potentially influencing the course of events. It serves as a cautionary note about the impact of public perception and the importance of managing narratives to ensure stability and control.

Quote 76

« Ordinarily men exercise their memory much more than their judgment. »

In the assertion "Ordinarily men exercise their memory much more than their judgment," Napoleon observes a common tendency where individuals prioritize the recollection of information over the critical evaluation of that information. He implies that people often rely on past experiences and established knowledge without critically analyzing or questioning the validity of their beliefs. Napoleon's insight highlights the cognitive inclination to rely on familiar patterns and preconceived notions, potentially leading to a limited scope of understanding. This sentiment underscores the importance of cultivating analytical thinking and the capacity to assess information with discernment, enabling individuals to make more informed decisions and gain a deeper grasp of the complexities of the world around them.

Quote 77

« I know he's a good general, but is he lucky? »

In the phrase "I know he's a good general, but is he lucky?" Napoleon Bonaparte encapsulates the role of chance and circumstances in determining outcomes, even in the context of skillful leadership. He implies that while competence and strategic prowess are essential, luck and fortuitous circumstances can play a significant role in achieving success. Napoleon's question underscores the acknowledgment that factors beyond one's control, often attributed to luck, can shape the course of events. This perspective reflects a pragmatic recognition of the unpredictable and multifaceted nature of achievements, suggesting that a combination of skill, strategy, and fortunate circumstances contribute to favorable outcomes.

Quote 78

« I am surrounded by priests who repeat incessantly that their kingdom is not of this world, and yet they lay hands on everything they can get. »

In the statement "I am surrounded by priests who repeat incessantly that their kingdom is not of this world, and yet they lay hands on everything they can get," Napoleon critiques the perceived hypocrisy within the religious hierarchy. He points out the incongruence between the professed spiritual focus of the clergy and their engagement in material pursuits. Napoleon suggests that some priests preach detachment from worldly possessions while simultaneously seeking to accumulate wealth and power. His observation underscores the tension between religious doctrine and human behavior, highlighting the contradictions that can arise when individuals prioritize their own interests over the principles they profess to uphold. This commentary reflects a skepticism about the authenticity of certain religious figures and their motivations.

Quote 79

« It is astonishing what power words have over men. »

In the declaration "It is astonishing what power words have over men," Napoleon Bonaparte underscores the profound impact of language and rhetoric on human thoughts, emotions, and actions. He suggests that words possess the ability to shape opinions, stir passions, and influence behaviors on a significant scale. This perspective reflects an awareness of the persuasive and manipulative potential of effective communication. Napoleon's observation highlights the role of language in shaping public sentiment, motivating individuals, and driving change, whether in the realms of politics, leadership, or interpersonal interactions. It emphasizes the critical importance of language as a tool for leaders to inspire, inform, and shape the perceptions of those they seek to influence.

Quote 80

« The fool has one great advantage over a man of sense — he is always satisfied with himself. »

In the assertion "The fool has one great advantage over a man of sense — he is always satisfied with himself," Napoleon contrasts the self-assuredness of individuals who lack discernment with those who possess intelligence and critical thinking. He implies that ignorance can lead to unwavering self-confidence, as fools may not be burdened by self-doubt or the complexities of self-reflection that more perceptive individuals grapple with. This perspective reflects a certain paradox, highlighting the potential drawbacks of excessive self-awareness and the ability of ignorance to create a sense of contentment. Napoleon's statement underscores the complexity of the relationship between knowledge, humility, and self-assurance, suggesting that the naive certainty of fools contrasts with the more nuanced perspectives of those who possess insight and understanding.

Quote 81

« History is the version of past events that
people have decided to agree upon. »

In the declaration "History is the version of past events
that people have decided to agree upon," Napoleon offers
a thought-provoking perspective on the construction of
historical narratives. He implies that historical accounts are
not absolute truths, but rather interpretations shaped by
collective consensus and societal perspectives. Napoleon's
statement reflects the malleability of history, as it is subject
to biases, political agendas, and cultural influences. This
observation underscores the complexities of constructing
an objective historical record and highlights how historical
narratives can be influenced, revised, or even manipulated
over time. It encourages a critical examination of historical
sources and a recognition of the inherent subjectivity in
how history is presented and understood.

Quote 82

« Men are Moved by two levers only: fear and self interest. »

In the assertion "Men are moved by two levers only: fear and self-interest," Napoleon Bonaparte encapsulates the basic drivers of human behavior. He suggests that the motivations of individuals are predominantly rooted in either the apprehension of negative consequences (fear) or the pursuit of personal gain and benefit (self-interest). Napoleon's observation simplifies the complex array of influences that guide human actions, underscoring the innate instincts that shape decision-making and interactions. This perspective reflects a pragmatic understanding of psychology, hinting at the underlying forces that propel individuals in their pursuits, interactions, and choices across various contexts.

Quote 83

« To understand the man you have to know what was happening in the world when he was twenty. »

In the statement "To understand the man you have to know what was happening in the world when he was twenty," Napoleon Bonaparte emphasizes the formative impact of a person's early experiences on their character and perspective. He suggests that understanding an individual requires insight into the historical, societal, and cultural context during their youth, as these factors contribute to shaping their beliefs, values, and worldview. Napoleon's observation underscores the idea that a person's upbringing and exposure to events during their formative years significantly influence their identity and subsequent life choices. This perspective underscores the enduring impact of one's environment on their development and serves as a reminder of the complexity of human nature.

Napoleon Bonaparte's
general quotes

Quote 84

« Greatness is nothing unless it be lasting. »

Napoleon's proclamation, "Greatness is nothing unless it be lasting," underscores the distinction between fleeting triumphs and enduring legacies. Through these words, he implies that temporary successes or short-lived accomplishments, no matter how grand, do not truly define greatness. Instead, true greatness is measured by its longevity and lasting impact. For Napoleon, who sought to reshape Europe and leave an indelible mark on history, the sentiment reflects the value he placed on long-term influence and legacy over momentary victories. His statement serves as a poignant reminder that the test of greatness lies not just in achieving glory, but in the ability to maintain and sustain it across the sands of time.

Quote 85

« You medical people will have more lives to answer for in the other world than even we generals. »

The statement, "You medical people will have more lives to answer for in the other world than even we generals," reflects a biting commentary on the responsibilities and potential failings of the medical profession. Napoleon, a general who was directly involved in warfare and its associated casualties, acknowledges the weight of his own responsibilities. Yet, he provocatively suggests that medical professionals, entrusted with the care and well-being of individuals, might bear even greater burdens for their mistakes or oversights. The remark underscores the gravity and significance of the medical profession's role, emphasizing that, in his view, their potential to harm—whether through negligence, lack of knowledge, or malpractice—could have consequences even weightier than the decisions made in the theater of war.

Quote 86

« If we could read the past histories of all our enemies we would disregard all hostility for them. »

In the declaration "If we could read the past histories of all our enemies we would disregard all hostility for them," Napoleon conveys the idea that a deeper understanding of an adversary's personal background and experiences could potentially engender empathy and diminish animosity. He suggests that if individuals were privy to the complex life stories and motivations of their enemies, they might find reasons to set aside hostility and instead cultivate a more compassionate perspective. This statement underscores the human tendency to perceive others solely through the lens of immediate conflict, neglecting the multifaceted histories and circumstances that contribute to an individual's actions.

Quote 87

« There is no such thing as accident; it is fate misnamed. »

In the assertion "There is no such thing as accident; it is fate misnamed," Napoleon Bonaparte challenges the concept of random chance and instead suggests that events often attributed to accidents are, in fact, manifestations of predetermined fate. He implies that the term "accident" merely serves as a label for occurrences that humans struggle to comprehend or explain within the framework of their understanding. Napoleon's perspective reflects a belief in the interconnectedness of events and a broader cosmic order that influences the unfolding of circumstances. By using the phrase "fate misnamed," he proposes that the apparent randomness of accidents might be better understood as part of a larger design or plan that transcends individual perception and control.

Quote 88

« Men are more easily governed through their vices than through their virtues. »

In the statement "Men are more easily governed through their vices than through their virtues," Napoleon Bonaparte suggests that individuals can be manipulated or controlled more effectively by exploiting their weaknesses and negative tendencies rather than by appealing to their positive qualities. He implies that human vulnerabilities, such as desires, fears, and selfish inclinations, can be harnessed to influence behavior and decisions. This observation reflects a pragmatic view of leadership and governance, highlighting the potential for those in positions of authority to leverage human frailties to achieve certain outcomes. Napoleon's perspective underscores the complexities of human psychology and the ways in which power can be wielded by understanding and manipulating human nature's less admirable aspects.

Quote 89

« It requires more courage
to suffer than to die. »

Reflecting on the complexities of the human spirit,
Napoleon Bonaparte once remarked, "It requires more
courage to suffer than to die." This statement encapsulates
the profound idea that while death is a singular, final event,
living through sustained pain or adversity demands an
ongoing reservoir of courage. Drawing from the crucible
of warfare and political strife, Napoleon understood the
myriad challenges people face, suggesting that enduring
life's trials often necessitates a deeper and more sustained
form of bravery than meeting death itself. Through this
lens, he celebrates the tenacity of the human spirit and the
quiet valor of enduring hardship.

Quote 90

« Let the path be open to talent. »

With the declaration "Let the path be open to talent," Napoleon Bonaparte emphasized the importance of meritocracy and the recognition of ability over birthright or privilege. In contrast to the deeply entrenched aristocratic systems of Europe, where social status and privilege were often determined by birth, Napoleon believed in elevating individuals based on their skills, achievements, and capabilities. This perspective was revolutionary for its time and marked a shift towards a more egalitarian approach to governance and societal structure. Napoleon's sentiment embodies the idea that talent should be the primary determinant of advancement, allowing societies to benefit from the full potential of their citizens, irrespective of their origins or social standings.

Quote 91

« He who knows how to flatter also knows how
to slander. »

In Napoleon's observation, "He who knows how to flatter also knows how to slander," speaks to the duality of human communication and the skill sets involved in both praise and deception. Napoleon suggests that those adept at crafting words to charm, praise, or appease others possess the same linguistic prowess to defame, deceive, or harm. The statement underscores the idea that eloquence is a double-edged sword, where the capacity to uplift with words carries with it the potential to destructively wield them. Within the context of the political and social spheres in which Napoleon operated, this insight emphasizes the need for discernment and caution when interpreting the intentions behind the words of those in power or seeking influence.

Quote 92

« One must learn to forgive and not to hold
a hostile, bitter attitude of mind, which
offends those about us and prevents us from
enjoying ourselves; one must recognize human
shortcomings and adjust himself to them rather
than to be constantly finding fault with them. »

In the statement "One must learn to forgive and not to hold a
hostile, bitter attitude of mind, which offends those about us
and prevents us from enjoying ourselves; one must recognize
human shortcomings and adjust himself to them rather than
to be constantly finding fault with them," Napoleon suggests
that harboring resentment or a negative outlook can create
a hostile atmosphere, hinder personal well-being, and strain
relationships. This insight encourages a compassionate
approach, advocating for understanding and acceptance of
human imperfections, which ultimately fosters harmony and
a more positive and fulfilling life. This perspective resonates
with the notion of emotional intelligence and the benefits of
cultivating a mindset of forgiveness and adaptability in
navigating the complexities of human
relationships.

Quote 93

« If you wish to be a success in the world,
promise everything, deliver nothing. »

Napoleon Bonaparte's saying, "If you wish to be a success
in the world, promise everything, deliver nothing," offers
a cynical perspective on the art of leadership and power
dynamics. Drawing from his observations of political
machinations and the nature of promises in the corridors of
power, Napoleon suggests that success—particularly in the
realm of politics or leadership—often involves manipulating
expectations. By promising everything, one can win
support, loyalty, or favor. Yet, by delivering nothing or only
a fraction of what's promised, one can maintain resources
and power without fully committing. This perspective,
while arguably Machiavellian, underscores the sometimes
duplicitous nature of power and the strategies employed by
those who seek to maintain or enhance
their positions.

Quote 94

« It is a mistake, too, to say that the face is the mirror of the soul. The truth is, men are very hard to know, and yet, not to be deceived, we must judge them by their present actions, but for the present only. »

In the statement "It is a mistake, too, to say that the face is the mirror of the soul. The truth is, men are very hard to know, and yet, not to be deceived, we must judge them by their present actions, but for the present only," Napoleon suggests that while understanding people can be challenging, the most accurate assessment comes from observing their current behaviors. He underscores the importance of recognizing that people evolve and that one's actions provide a more reliable basis for judgment, though he acknowledges the limitations in fully grasping the depth of individuals. This perspective encourages a balanced approach, considering both the unpredictability of human behavior and the practical need to make judgments based on observable actions.

Quote 95

« The people to fear are not those who disagree
with you, but those who disagree with you and
are too cowardly to let you know. »

In the assertion "The people to fear are not those who
disagree with you, but those who disagree with you and
are too cowardly to let you know," Napoleon highlights the
potential threat posed by individuals who withhold their
dissenting opinions due to fear or apprehension. He suggests
that open disagreement, even if contrary to one's own views,
demonstrates a level of courage and integrity, as it allows for
open dialogue and the potential for mutual understanding.
Napoleon's observation underscores the importance of
transparent communication and the value of diverse
perspectives, cautioning against those who may harbor
hidden agendas or motivations. This perspective encourages
an environment where differing viewpoints can be
expressed openly, fostering healthy debate and
a more informed decision-making process.

Quote 96

« There is no place in a fanatic's head where
reason can enter. »

In the statement "There is no place in a fanatic's head
where reason can enter," Napoleon Bonaparte alludes to the
unyielding nature of fanaticism and its resistance to rational
discourse. He suggests that individuals consumed by extreme
beliefs or ideologies often close themselves off from logical
reasoning and critical thinking. Napoleon's observation
underscores the challenging nature of engaging in productive
conversations with fanatics, as their steadfast devotion to
their beliefs may hinder their ability to consider alternative
viewpoints. This perspective serves as a cautionary note
about the limitations of engaging in rational discussions
with individuals who have embraced extreme ideologies,
emphasizing the importance of recognizing when
constructive dialogue may be futile and seeking
more effective means of communication.

Quote 97

« With audacity one can undertake anything,
but not do everything. »

In the declaration "With audacity one can undertake anything, but not do everything," Napoleon Bonaparte encapsulates the power of boldness and initiative in embarking on ambitious endeavors. He suggests that possessing the courage to take risks and push boundaries can open doors to numerous possibilities and opportunities. However, he also underscores the practical limitation that even audacity has its boundaries; while it enables the initiation of ventures, it doesn't guarantee the ability to execute all plans successfully. Napoleon's perspective underscores the need for strategic thinking, calculated risk-taking, and the recognition that audacity is a powerful tool in the realm of initiation but must be coupled with careful planning and resourcefulness to achieve sustainable outcomes.

Quote 98

« All great events hang by a single thread. The clever man takes advantage of everything, neglects nothing that may give him some added opportunity; the less clever man, by neglecting one thing, sometimes misses everything. »

In the statement "All great events hang by a single thread. The clever man takes advantage of everything, neglects nothing that may give him some added opportunity; the less clever man, by neglecting one thing, sometimes misses everything," Napoleon suggests that significant outcomes often hinge on a fragile and pivotal element, where astute individuals seize every possible advantage and opportunity to enhance their chances. Napoleon's insight highlights the importance of meticulous attention to detail and strategic thinking in identifying and capitalizing on potential avenues for success. Conversely, he emphasizes the risks of overlooking seemingly minor factors, which can have far-reaching consequences. This perspective underscores the nuanced interplay between preparedness, opportunism, and the interconnected nature of events in achieving desired results.

Quote 99

« It is my wish that my ashes may repose on the banks of the Seine, in the midst of the French people, whom I have loved so well. »

In the declaration "It is my wish that my ashes may repose on the banks of the Seine, in the midst of the French people, whom I have loved so well," Napoleon Bonaparte expresses a poignant desire to remain close to the heart of the nation he served and led. He signifies a deep emotional attachment to France and its people, reflecting his sentiment of affection and dedication to the country he shaped and defended. Napoleon's words evoke a sense of nostalgia and a yearning for a lasting connection to his homeland, reflecting his profound bond with the land and the people he considered his own. This sentiment encapsulates the profound relationship between a leader and the land they govern, revealing a desire for a final resting place that symbolically unites his legacy with the nation's history.

Quote 100

« What is history but a fable agreed upon? »

In the assertion "What is history but a fable agreed upon?" Napoleon Bonaparte presents a thought-provoking perspective on the nature of historical narratives. He implies that historical accounts are not necessarily objective truths, but rather stories that have been shaped and accepted by consensus over time. Napoleon's statement underscores the malleability of historical interpretation, highlighting the potential for biases, political agendas, and societal influences to shape the way events are remembered and portrayed. This observation encourages critical examination of historical sources and a recognition of the subjectivity inherent in constructing and perceiving history. It prompts contemplation on the complex interplay between the past, present, and the way collective memory is curated and passed down.

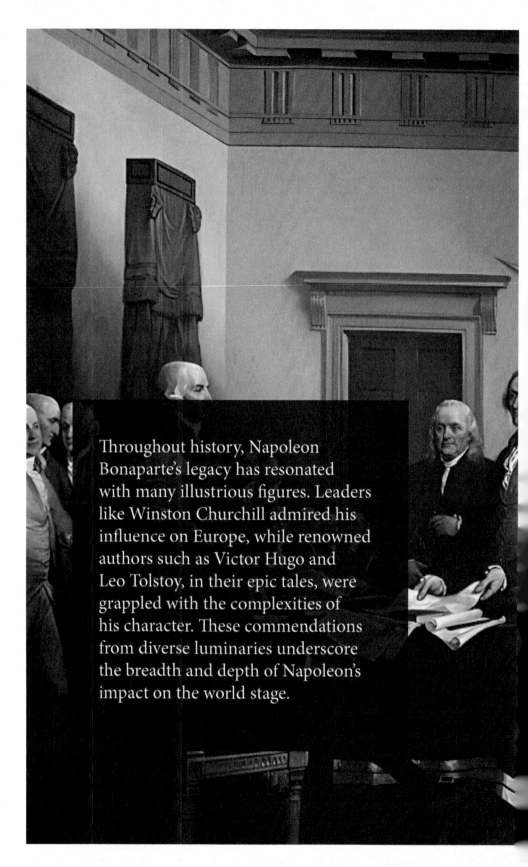

Throughout history, Napoleon Bonaparte's legacy has resonated with many illustrious figures. Leaders like Winston Churchill admired his influence on Europe, while renowned authors such as Victor Hugo and Leo Tolstoy, in their epic tales, were grappled with the complexities of his character. These commendations from diverse luminaries underscore the breadth and depth of Napoleon's impact on the world stage.

chapter 3

Honorable Mentions

Ludwig von Beethoven

1770 - 1827

musician

« So he is no more than a common mortal ! Now, too, he will tread under foot all the rights of man, indulge only his ambition; now he will think himself superior to all men, become a tyrant ! »

Beethoven admired Napoleon for his democratic ideals and initially dedicated his "Eroica" Symphony to him.

Johann Wolfgang von Goethe

1749 - 1832

poet

« I was much struck with his clear, beautiful and penetrating eyes, from which I could not withdraw my own. »

Goethe and Napoleon met in 1808 in Erfurt, expressing mutual admiration, with Napoleon revealing his deep respect for Goethe's literary genius and Goethe being impressed by Napoleon's vision and charisma.

Jacques-Louis David

1748 - 1825

painter

« What a beautiful head he has! It is pure …
beautiful like (the) antique. »

Jacques-Louis David was Napoleon Bonaparte's
official court painter, immortalizing the
emperor's image in iconic artworks like
"Napoleon Crossing the Alps."

Adolf Hitler

1889 - 1945

politician / dictator

« Napoleon was a titan, and his battles are more eternal than the most beautiful cathedrals in Europe. »

Adolf Hitler admired Napoleon Bonaparte for his strategic genius and empire-building, often drawing parallels between their ambitions for European dominance.

Winston Churchill

1874 - 1965

prime minister of UK

« Of all the tyrants in history, Napoleon was the
most gifted. »

Winston Churchill studied and wrote about
Napoleon, recognizing his military genius while
also critiquing his imperial ambitions.

Leo Tolstoy

1828 - 1910

writer

« He did not, or did not wish to, understand the meaning of the event at the moment of its occurrence. »

Leo Tolstoy, in his novel "War and Peace," critically portrayed Napoleon Bonaparte, contrasting the emperor's ambition with the Russian spirit and individual destinies affected by the grand sweep of history.

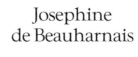

Josephine
de Beauharnais

1763 - 1814

empress / napoleon's wife

« If what I am to you, monsieur, has aided you
in becoming great, I hail the event with joy.
If I could have been of service to you without
belonging to you, I would have preferred it. »

Napoleon and Josephine's turbulent romance,
marked by passion, infidelity, and political
intrigue, became one of history's most iconic and
complex love stories.

« A man like me cares little about losing the lives
of a million men. »

Napoleon Bonaparte, driven by boundless
ambition and a keen sense of his own historical
significance, was both his greatest advocate and
harshest critic.

Dear Reader,

If you had a good time reading,
please consider leaving a review
on Amazon for this book.
It would mean super much to me!

Thank you very much!

—— **Hannah B.**

Napoleon Revealed

44 Famous Paintings & Quotes

Printed in Great Britain
by Amazon